Making European Wines at Home

Making European Wines at Home

Taste the Vineyards of the World with 133 Delicious Wines That Can Be Made in Your Kitchen

Bryan Acton & Peter Duncan

Copyright © Bryan Acton and Peter Duncan, 1964, 2011.

First published in the United Kingdom by Amateur Winemaker Publications, 1964.
First published in North America in 2011, updated and revised, by Fox Chapel Publishing, 1970 Broad Street, East Petersburg, PA 17520.

All rights reserved. No part of this publication may be reproduced, stored in a retrieval system, or transmitted, in any form or by any means, electronic, mechanical, photocopying, recording or otherwise, without prior permission of the copyright holder.

ISBN 978-1-56523-674-5

Library of Congress Cataloging-in-Publication Data

Acton, George William Bryan.
 Making European wines at home / Bryan Acton and Peter Duncan. -- [Updated and rev.].
   p. cm.
 Rev. ed. of: Making wines like those you buy. 1964.
 Includes index.
 ISBN 978-1-56523-674-5
 1. Wine and wine making--Amateurs' manuals. I. Duncan, Peter, 1937- II. Acton, George William Bryan. Making wines like those you buy. III. Title.
 TP548.2.A258 2011
 641.87'2094--dc23
                               2011020157

To learn more about the other great books from Fox Chapel Publishing, or to find a retailer near you, call toll-free 800-457-9112 or visit us at *www.FoxChapelPublishing.com*.

Note to Authors: We are always looking for talented authors to write new books. Please send a brief letter describing your idea to Acquisition Editor, 1970 Broad Street, East Petersburg, PA 17520.

Printed in Indonesia
First printing: December 2011

Because working with fermenting liquids and other materials inherently includes the risk of injury and damage, this book cannot guarantee that using the recipes in this book is safe for everyone. For this reason, this book is sold without warranties or guarantees of any kind, expressed or implied, and the publisher and the author disclaim any liability for any injuries, losses, or damages caused in any way by the content of this book or the reader's use of the ingredients needed to complete the recipes presented here. The publisher and the author urge all readers to thoroughly review each project and to understand the effects of all ingredients before starting any recipe.

TABLE OF CONTENTS

Introduction 6

Chapter 1: Basic Winemaking 8

Chapter 2: Sherry (dry and sweet) 22

Chapter 3: Port 32

Chapter 4: Hocks, Moselles, and Alsatian Wines 40

Chapter 5: Dry Red Wines of France 48

Chapter 6: White Wines of France 56

Chapter 7: Chianti (new and old) 68

Chapter 8: Madeira-Type Wines 74

Chapter 9: Rosé Wines 82

Chapter 10: Champagne and Sparkling Wines 90

Chapter 11: Liqueurs and Aperitifs 100

Index 126

INTRODUCTION

Thousands of people make wine, much of it excellent, and many are content just to produce their own country wines (and drink them!). But winemaking, like any other worthwhile pursuit, contains an element of challenge, and to the serious winemaker, the ultimate challenge is to be able to reproduce from his own resources the famous wine types of the world, at a fraction of their normal cost.

Your true winemaker must gradually become, to however slight a degree, a student of commercial wines, and it is inevitable that, eventually, he will wish to make homemade wines like those he buys and loves. He can do it the easiest way of all, of course, by buying one of the many kits now on the market, which vary widely both in price and quality. They reduce winemaking to its ultimate simplicity, but, as any winemaker knows, they are far more expensive than wine produced from garden or wild fruit, and sometimes not nearly as good. So the easy way is also the expensive way.

Making European Wines at Home tells you in detailed fashion how to do the job with your own ingredients, at minimal cost and with maximum satisfaction.

All recipes are given for either 5-quart (4.5-liter) or 22.5-quart (20-liter) quantities, because it is believed that many winemakers of experience will prefer the larger quantity.

This book also contains full and comprehensive instructions on the making of liqueurs, because producing them at home greatly alleviates their expense.

There is no doubt that Bryan Acton and Peter Duncan have between them produced what has become the accepted textbook for these specialized aspects of our enthralling hobby.

—C. J. J. Berry

Chapter 1

BASIC WINEMAKING

The title of this book, *Making European Wines at Home*, was deliberately chosen.

There have been a great many books on winemaking since it became such a popular hobby and most of them have been concerned either with the techniques involved or with recipes for country wines. This little book differs from the others in that it boldly sets out to help produce wines that compare with those you might drink in Europe.

Until fairly recently, the average person had but little appreciation of the virtues of wine. It is still not uncommon to hear someone say, "We had a nice bottle of Port at Christmas time," a statement that contrasts violently with the amateur winemaker's, "I bottled sixty bottles of Elderberry Port last night." The real appreciation of wine came when people started to flock to Europe for the holidays. They make very poor tea abroad, if at all, and the warm climate no longer makes coffee such a satisfactory thirst quencher. Instead, one of the best drinks you can purchase is wine.

It is good honest wine, gallons and gallons of it pouring down millions of eager throats in an endless torrent and with very satisfactory results to one's state of contentment. It is curious that with all the sightseeing tours undertaken abroad, the only lasting memories are often of friendly cafés with good wine and some music that produced a state of inner peace reached but rarely in life.

Affording Wine Daily

We will suppose you are a wine lover. Why else, indeed, would you be reading this? If you were wealthy enough, you would have a great cellar crammed full of the choicest wines. This is the region of daydreaming and what better way to spend an evening than browsing through a wine magazine (with a glass of wine in one's hand) and to furnish an imaginary cellar with ports, Madeiras, Sauternes, clarets, and so on? The cost of actually doing this would, of course, be quite prohibitive for most of us, and when one comes down to earth, it is in the cheaper sections of the magazine that one starts to look. If one cannot afford Montrachet then perhaps Macon Blanc will have to do. But even these are expensive if one wants to drink wine regularly. A bottle of cheap wine a day will run up quite a yearly bill. Wine kits will reduce the expense, but what this book offers is a bottle of wine a day for a fraction of the cost, utilizing fruits from garden and fields.

BUT WHAT OF THE QUALITY?

It is a curious fact that homemade cakes are valued as being much better than store-bought cakes, while the reverse is the case when wines are considered. Unfortunately, in the past, this was indeed the correct position. The literary scorn of our "abominable rustic concoctions" was generally justified, for only in the realm of mead, cider, beer, and whiskey did homebrewers excel. For the most part, many home-produced wines were off-flavored parsnip wines, sharp elderflower wines, and other oversweet cordials far removed from the excellent wines of Europe.

The impact of science (which is only knowledge, after all!) on winemaking has produced a revolution that has made it possible for wines to be made that resemble those of France, Italy, and Germany. Many winemakers using these new techniques still prefer to make country wines, and their wines are very much higher in quality than those of their ancestors.

HOW GOOD ARE THESE WINES GOING TO BE?

An honest answer to this question is that if you pay attention to everything in this book, about 80 percent of the wines you produce will be as good as the wines you buy in the cheaper ranges of commercial wines and about 10 percent will be of such excellent quality that they will not be disgraced in the company of more expensive commercial wines. About 10 percent may be disappointing, and we can afford to accept that number. We do not claim that with the ingredients we use, or in the smaller quantities we make, we can match the best of commercial wines. Such wines as Chambertin in the Burgundies, vintage port, Chateau d'Yquem in the Sauternes, Chateau Latour in the clarets, and the best hocks and Moselles stand in a class of their own, and always will.

Having said that, however, let us illustrate the point with a story. The former editor of *Amateur Winemaker* magazine Mr. Cyril J. J. Berry once sent a couple of bottles of his own wine across to some friends in France with whom his daughter Gay was staying. The French friends, themselves extremely knowledgeable about wine, so valued this wine that they rated it as a liqueur and served it to their friends as such on special occasions. This demonstrates the excellent quality wines you can make from a mixture of such ingredients as apricots, grape concentrate, elderberries, and bananas. Don't be overawed by wine snobs and connoisseurs. The whole purpose of this book is to allow you to make good honest everyday wines for your table and for social drinking.

Basic Knowledge

We would like to bring to your notice at this point another book that, if you are a beginner and intensely interested in winemaking, you would do well to acquire: *First Steps in Winemaking*. This book assumes you have a basic working knowledge of the winemaking process and will successfully be able to follow the given recipes with little aid from us. If you are a true beginner, however, with the aid of *First Steps in Winemaking*, you can come to know the reasons behind the recipes, be able to design your own recipes, in time, and in every sense of the word, be able to call yourself a craftsman in wine.

HOW WINE IS MADE

For those who are beginner winemakers, we will outline in non-technical language just how an alcoholic drink such as wine comes to be made.

Yeasts are some of nature's "demolition engineers." It is their job to break down vegetable matter into its basic elements so that life can renew itself again from these materials. This is what happens in a compost heap in the garden or when a fruit salad starts to go bad in the fridge.

Yeast, however, can do one thing human beings cannot do. If our air supply is cut off, we die, but if the air supply of yeast is cut off, it can go on living, provided a supply of sugar is available. The yeast breaks down the sugar into alcohol, carbon dioxide gas, and energy (the latter being what the yeast requires to live and grow).

All a winemaker does, basically, is take a mixture of sugar and fruit juice (generally diluted with water), add yeast, which is a living organism, and allow the yeast colony to grow with plenty of air. Then the winemaker cuts off the air supply and allows the yeast to attack the sugar, producing alcohol. In every 5 quarts (4.5 liters) of must (the initial sugar/fruit juice mixture), every pound of sugar dissolved will furnish the wine with about 5 percent alcohol by volume (about 9 proof spirit). Even yeast cannot go on forever, though, and when the alcohol tolerance of the yeast is reached, fermentation stops, the yeast dies, and the wine starts to clear and become stable. This is why most yeast is unable to produce more than 16-18 percent alcohol except under rare conditions.

WHY WE USE MIXTURES OF INGREDIENTS

Of all the fruits in the world, the grape is supreme for winemaking. It has (when at its best) the ideal balance of sugar, acid, tannin, and so on, which can produce a fine balanced wine. In Britain, very few, if any, of our fruits and none of our vegetables are as balanced as the grape. By blending a number of ingredients into a composite fruit/vegetable juice mixture, we can arrive at a balance that is, in most cases, as good as that possessed by the grape. If you find one of the ingredients is not available, try to substitute in a similar fruit or vegetable to ensure the proper balance is maintained.

Ordinary granulated sugar is intended for use in the wines mentioned in our recipes. There are many other forms of sugar, some with unwanted flavors of their own, but they all behave the same way in the presence of yeast in a well-balanced must.

What is important, however, is that sugar should be added to a must in syrup form, little by little, as indicated in the recipes. In high-alcohol wines, this allows the yeast to increase its tolerance of alcohol, making the finished wine higher in alcohol than it would otherwise be.

Another important note is that when a wine has finished fermenting and has been racked (siphoned off its yeast deposit), no further sugar should be added *at that point*. Adding sugar at that time tends to produce a very minute continued fermentation, which will prevent the wine from clearing rapidly. Wines should be sweetened, if desired, when they are completely stable, not immediately after fermentation.

DOUBLE YOUR MONEY'S WORTH

If you are following one of the recipes for a dessert wine, particularly with fruit such as elderberries, bilberries, plums, and damsons (fruits with a great deal of color), it is sometimes possible to get two wines from the same fruit. One of these is the heavy-bodied dessert wine indicated in the recipe and the other is a light table wine.

In most of these cases, the recipe will advocate fermenting on the pulp for a few days, after which the pulp is strained off. At this point, the pulp (if sound and holding together well) can be placed in another fermenting bin. Two pounds (900 grams) of sugar per 5 quarts (4.5 liters) and ¾ ounces (25 grams) of acid per 5 quarts (4.5 liters) should be added, the liquid content restored with water at 70°-75°F (20°-25°C), and the fermentation allowed to continue. The pulp can be strained off a couple of days later, resulting in a light table wine of the rosé type.

Basic Winemaking

EQUIPMENT

The very minimum of equipment required is:

- A polyethylene 10-quart (9-liter) bucket (fermenting vessel)
- A glass jar or demijohn
- A polyethylene funnel
- A nylon sieve
- A piece of rubber tubing about a yard long
- A piece of glass tubing bent into a small *u* at one end (siphon tube)
- Additional glass jars or polypins to hold wine in bulk as one's winemaking proceeds
- Fermentation locks (devices that allow the carbon dioxide to bubble off while preventing the entry of bacteria)
- A hydrometer and trial jar (see *Using the hydrometer*)
- Metal and enamel containers (used for boiling ingredients where indicated, but never for fermentation, as metallic hazes and perhaps poisons can be released into the wine)

BEGINNER'S *VIN ORDINAIRE*

We have said earlier that it would be advisable to obtain and read *First Steps in Winemaking* if you are an absolute beginner. It is always better to know why you are doing things rather than following recipes blindly. In the meantime, however, you want to get on with the winemaking as quickly as possible, and may not even want to wait long enough to obtain the wine yeast, nutrients, and so on used in later recipes. What you want is a quick trip to the nearest supermarket for one or two ingredients, stopping at the winemaker's supply store for some yeast, and straight home to make wine. While it is not possible to produce a top-quality wine under these conditions, because it will lack certain balancing ingredients and you are unlikely to leave it long enough to mature before drinking it, it should nevertheless compare relatively well with the rough local wine you might encounter in some bars. It will, in fact, usually be stronger in alcohol. We assume you have the basic equipment mentioned, so the ingredients you need are:

- Two 12-oz. (375-g.) packets of raisins or sultanas (seedless white grapes)
- 20-fl.-oz. (550-ml.) tin of fruit juice (orange, apple, or pineapple)
- 2 lb. (900 g.) granulated sugar
- 1 lemon
- Dried baker's yeast—do not use brewer's yeast or your wine will pick up the flavor

METHOD:

1. Boil the sugar with 20 fl. oz. (570 ml.) of water for a few minutes until the solution becomes crystal clear. Allow it to cool and store in a bottle for the time being.
2. Wash out your plastic bucket well with plain water.
3. Chop the raisins or put them through a mincer and place them in the bucket.
4. Next, add the juice of the lemon, the fruit juice, and 20 fl. oz. (570 ml.) of the sugar syrup.
5. Boil 6 pints (2.85 liters) of water and add it, boiling, to the bucket. Stir well until everything is well mixed.
6. Cover the bucket with a blanket or piece of polyethylene and allow it to cool to room temperature (around 70°F, 20°C). This is of the utmost importance, for if

the yeast is added when the temperature is above 80°F (27°C), it may become seriously weakened.

7. When the must is at room temperature, add a teaspoonful of the yeast, stir well, cover the bucket again, and keep at a temperature of 70°-75°F (20°-25°C).

8. Look at the must occasionally, without completely uncovering the plastic bucket. When the raisins come up to the surface all together, the fermentation has commenced. This may take a few hours or a few days, so be patient.

9. We will call the day on which fermentation starts Day 1, and the procedure then continues as follows:
   a) Day 1-4: Stir the brew twice daily, replacing the cover each time.
   b) Day 5: Strain the wine off the pulp through a nylon sieve into the demijohn jar. Add 5 fl. oz. (150 ml.) of the sugar syrup, shake the jar or stir the contents with the handle of a wooden spoon to mix the syrup in well, and then plug the jar with a firm wad of cotton wool.
   c) Day 6: Leave the wine for the day.
   d) Day 7: Add 5 fl. oz. (150 ml.) of sugar syrup, stirring it in well as before, and replace the cotton wool plug.
   e) Day 8: Leave the wine for the day.
   f) Day 9: Taste the wine. Ignore the current unpalatable flavor, tasting instead for sweetness.
   If there is little sweetness apparent, add another 5 fl. oz. (150 ml.) of sugar syrup, mix well, and replace the plug. If the wine still tastes sweet, delay the sugar addition for two days.
   g) Day 10-11: Leave the wine for the day.
   h) Day 12: Repeat the procedure for Day 9. This sugar addition will use up the last of your syrup. Do not be surprised if this last addition cannot be added for several days, because the yeast is reaching the point at which its further growth will be inhibited by the alcohol present. Temperature will also affect the rate of fermentation. Never add any sugar until the yeast has used up that already added, or you may be left with an oversweet wine.

10. The wine should now be left for another two weeks to finish its fermentation, and when it no longer tastes sweet and only a few bubbles are rising to the surface, it has to be racked, i.e., poured off the sediment of yeast and pulp debris. If you have a second demijohn, this should be used, but otherwise six wine bottles or other containers can be used. If you have some rubber tubing, the wine can be siphoned off carefully so the siphon tube is not too close to the sediment, otherwise it must be carefully poured. Stop pouring if any sediment starts to flow into the new container, reseal both jars with cotton wool, and wait a few hours before pouring again. Finally, top off the new jar with tap water until it is completely full and plug it with a bored cork or a very tight wad of cotton wool. Place the jar in a cool place.

11. Have a look at the jar after about two weeks. If a fine sediment of yeast has formed, everything is all right. If, on the other hand, a thick sediment forms (say over ¼ in., 5 mm., thick) or, particularly, if a two-tone sediment

occurs (light brown yeast and yellowish-green fruit pulp), rack the wine once more and again top off with tap water and reseal the jar.

12. Now you must be patient, not disturbing the wine or tasting it for three months.

13. After three months, rack the wine and sweeten it up to your own taste with sugar syrup (normally 5 fl. oz. (150 ml.) or 10 fl. oz. (280 ml.) of syrup is sufficient). Make the syrup by boiling ½ lb. (225 g.) of sugar with 5 fl. oz. (150 ml.) of water. You will find that this makes a distinct improvement to the wine, and if it is your first wine, you will probably drink it at this stage. It should really be kept another three months at least. This is not a wine that merits bottling, so fill up your decanters from the jar and good health, you have become a winemaker!

TEMPERATURE

While commercial experts still disagree on the optimum temperature for fermentation, it has been found that 70°-75°F (20°-35°C) is suitable for most purposes. Avoid temperatures above 80°F (27°C). At very low temperatures, the fermentation slows or even stops. Certain yeasts are designed to operate at low temperatures and will sometimes continue a very slow fermentation in unheated rooms in the winter.

PECTIC ENZYME

This is an enzyme, obtainable from all winemaking suppliers, which will destroy pectin. Where quoted in recipes, it will assist the rapid clarification of certain wines.

HOW TO PREPARE A YEAST STARTER

1. Take a clean wine bottle and sterilize it with the stock sulfite solution.

2. When the bottle is sterilized, rinse it out with tap water and plug it with cotton wool.

3. Boil up one of the following mixtures in a saucepan (with a lid) and allow it to cool (with the lid remaining on):
    a) 1 tablespoon (10 ml.) malt extract, 1 tablespoon (10 ml.) sugar, ½ heaping teaspoon (5 ml.) citric acid, 2 cups water
    b) Juice of two oranges, 1 tablespoon (10 ml.) sugar, 2 cups water
    c) 1 cup of the fruit juice that will be fermented, 1 cup water, 1 tablespoon (10 ml.) sugar

4. When mixture is at room temperature, pour it into a bottle, add yeast, and replace the cotton wool. Many types of modern wine yeast can be added in this way without any prior preparation. Keep that jar at about 75°F (25°C).

5. Agar cultures and liquid yeast will normally start fermenting in a matter of hours, but some types of yeast, in particular dried yeast, may take several days.

6. A further 24 hours should elapse before adding the culture to the main must if such a wait is possible.

7. If only two-thirds of the culture is added to the must and the starter bottle is topped up with a fresh sterile starter mixture, the starter can be used many times before being rejected. In between uses, store the starter in a refrigerator and only bring it into warmer rooms a few hours before being used.

8. Some of the finest types of wine yeast are sold in test-tube form, the yeast being on an agar slant. Many amateur winemakers have difficulty slipping the agar jelly slant out of the test tube. An alternative method is to immerse the test tube in the stock sulfite solution (to sterilize the outside of the test tube), rinse it with tap water, unplug it, and drop the entire test tube into the starter bottle. Tilting the bottle slightly will ensure the starter mixture fills up the test tube, which can be extracted when the starter is added to the must.

USING THE HYDROMETER

It would be out of place to give a detailed account of the hydrometer in a book of this nature. We intend, therefore, to highlight two of its uses that are helpful to winemakers.

The hydrometer is simply a weighted hollow tube containing a graduated scale. It is floated in a liquid (which is first poured into a suitable test jar), and the depth to which the hydrometer sinks gives a measure of how much sugar the liquid contains.

Knowing how much sugar can be added to a fermenting wine, and at what rate, is the beginner's main problem. The secret to success is to take hydrometer readings of your wine about every two days and to wait until the reading has fallen to 10 (1.010) or below before adding further sugar during the first two weeks of fermentation. Sugar can then be added at the rate of ¼ pound (110 grams) per 5 quarts (4.5 liters) each time the reading falls to 10. If the sugar syrup is made up as instructed in the recipes, every 5 fluid ounces (150 milliliters) of syrup contains ¼ pound (110 grams) of sugar.

Basic Winemaking

Specific gravity	Specific gravity abbreviation	Weight of sugar (grams in 4.5 liters)	Weight of sugar (ounces in 5 quarts)
1.000	0	0	0
1.005	5	28.5	1
1.010	10	57	2
1.015	15	113	4
1.020	20	198	7
1.025	25	256	9
1.030	30	340	12
1.035	35	425	15
1.040	40	481	17
1.045	45	538	19
1.050	50	595	21
1.055	55	652	23
1.060	60	708	25
1.065	65	765	27
1.070	70	822	29
1.075	75	878	31
1.080	80	935	33
1.085	85	1020	36
1.090	90	1077	38
1.095	95	1134	40
1.100	100	1190	42
1.105	105	1247	44
1.110	110	1304	46
1.115	115	1360	48
1.120	120	1417	50
1.125	125	1474	52
1.130	130	1530	54
1.135	135	1587	56
1.140	140		
1.145	145		
1.150	150		
1.155	155		
1.160	160		

After about two weeks, the reading can be allowed to go down to 0 (1.000) or below before more sugar syrup is added.

The second problem, that of ascertaining how much alcohol a wine contains, is a little more complicated. There is no method that is both easy and accurate.

The following method gives a close approximation. It is about the simplest method to use and, largely corrects the effect of substances other than sugar dissolved in the must, which affect specific gravity readings. Do not mix measurements; work wholly in liters or wholly in quarts.

1. Take a specific gravity reading of your initial must.
2. Read from the previous table the weight of sugar in 5 quarts (4.5 liters) that corresponds to this specific gravity.
3. Calculate from this the amount of sugar in the number of quarts or liters you actually have initially (not the number you intend to make).
4. Add to this figure all the weight of sugar you add to the must during the course of fermentation (remember, 20 fl. oz. (570 ml.) of sugar syrup equals 1 lb. (450 g.) of sugar).
5. Divide this total of sugar by the number of quarts or liters of finished wine and, from the table, read back the specific gravity corresponding to that weight of sugar.
6. Take the specific gravity of the finished wine and deduct it from the specific gravity just read.
7. Divide this specific gravity drop by 7.5. The result is the percentage of alcohol by volume in your wine.
8. If you want the figure in proof spirit, multiply the percentage by volume by 1.75.

AN EXAMPLE:

Say you have 3.75 quarts (3.4 liters) of must with a specific gravity of 35 (1.035).

The table shows that a must with this specific gravity reading has the sugar equivalent of 15 oz. (425 g.) per 5 quarts (4.5 liters). At this rate, your must contains about 11.25 oz. (319 g.) of sugar.

You will add about 40 fl. oz. (1150 ml.) of sugar syrup in the course of fermentation, or 32 oz. (900 g.) sugar.

You total sugar is therefore about 43.25 oz. (1219 g.), giving you a specific gravity reading of about 104 if you are making 5 quarts of wine.

Say the final gravity reading was 0.995.

Deduct 995 from 1104, representing a gravity drop of 109.

After dividing 109 by 7.5, you will find that your wine is about 14.5 percent alcohol by volume or 25 proof spirit.

ACID

Acid is essential for a balanced fermentation, for the production of flavor during a wine's maturation, and for its own effect on the palate, without which a wine would taste insipid. Generalizing somewhat, a dry wine requires about 3 parts per thousand (ppt) acid and a sweet wine about 4 ppt (expressed in terms of the European standard, sulfuric acid, which is, of course, never actually used in winemaking).

The recipes in this book have been worked out to reflect the correct acidity, and the correct balance of acids where possible, but, being recipes, they have the fault that they cannot take into account changing climatic conditions. In a very long hot summer, the acidity of fruits falls below estimates, while in a very poor unseasonable summer, acidity exceeds estimates.

Because of this, it is advisable to check the acidity of your wine musts and to adjust them to the correct figure. You can usually find testing kits in your local winemaking store. These kits test acid content, sugar content, starch hazes, and pectin hazes.

SULFUR DIOXIDE

Sulfur dioxide has been used in commercial winemaking since time immemorial. Amateur winemakers now use sulfur dioxide also, either in the form of Campden tablets or as potassium metabisulfite or sodium metabisulfite, better known to winemakers simply as sulfite. Campden tablets are the most practical for the winemaker who makes only the occasional gallon of wine, each tablet representing 50 parts per million (ppm) sulfur dioxide.

More expensive winemaking requires some regard for the cost of subsidiary chemicals used, and it is more economical to purchase 1 pound (about 500 grams) of sodium metabisulfite from a winemaking supply store and make it into a stock solution. To make the solution, pour the metabisulfite crystals into a 5-quart (4.5-liter) jar, add 3.75 pints (about 2 liters) warm water, and shake the jar until the crystals are dissolved. Top off the jar to the 5-quart (4.5-liter) mark with cold tap water. The fumes that arise from this solution are the same choking fumes that occur in smog, so care should be taken not to inhale these during mixing or in later use of the solution.

SOME USES FOR SULFITE:

1. When a fermentation is started in which no heat or boiling water have been used in the preparation of the must, 100 ppm of sulfite should be added to every 5 quarts (4.5 liters) of must (2 Campden tablets or 1 tablespoon, 10 milliliters, stock solution). The yeast should be added 24 hours later. This procedure will kill off or inhibit the activity of harmful bacteria without unduly slowing down yeast activity, and will assist in the production of small amounts of glycerol. In addition, the flavoring esters of the ingredients are now

contained in the must instead of having been driven off by heat or boiling water.

2. When racking wines, particularly white wines, the racked wine should be treated with 50 ppm sulfur dioxide (1 Campden tablet or ½ teaspoon, 5 milliliters, stock solution) per 5 quarts (4.5 liters). This procedure helps prevent wine from becoming over-oxidized due to too much aeration and ensures better maturing.

This process can be repeated at every racking without any danger of sulfite building up in the wine.

3. The sterilization of jars, bottles, and corks should always be carried out with the aid of sulfite. The stock solution is most satisfactory for this, and about 20 fluid ounces (550 milliliters) of solution should be put into a separate bottle for this purpose. To sterilize a jar, the solution is simply poured into the jar, the jar is swirled around, and then the solution is poured back into its original bottle. Twenty fluid ounces (550 milliliters) of solution, although becoming discolored in its use, will normally last several months. As long as the sulfur dioxide can be smelled, the solution is active. Bottles can also be sterilized in the same way, by pouring the solution from bottle to bottle. Corks can be placed in the funnel used during bottle sterilization and be cleaned at the same time.

4. The stock solution can be diluted by nine times its own volume to provide a solution that is useful for mopping up spilled wine and large-scale disinfection of the winery.

POSSIBLE TROUBLES

Using the recipes in this book, one should but rarely encounter wines that remain persistently hazy even after several months maturing. In compiling the recipes, we have avoided using materials that might cause hazes or have called for the use of haze-destroying enzymes in recipes where we anticipated a haze might occur.

The following summary of the principal causes, detection, and treatment of hazy wines may, however, be of use on some occasions. It is as well to wait several months before deciding that a wine has a persistent haze.

Pectin haze: This is the most common type of haze. To test for pectin, take one volume of wine and add four volumes of methylated spirits to it. Allow this to stand for half an hour. If pectin is present, jellylike clots and strings will form. Treat the wine with ½ ounce (15 grams) of a pectic enzyme per 5 quarts (4.5 liters) and bring it into a warm room for about a week.

Starch hazes: These hazes occur in grain wines and wines made from apples and similar fruits. Test for starch by taking a glass of the wine and adding a few drops of iodine. If starch is present, the wine will turn indigo blue. Treat the wine with ½ ounce (15 grams) of amylase per 5 quarts (4.5 liters) and bring it into a warm place. (Amylase can be obtained from most amateur winemaking suppliers.)

Non-depositing yeast hazes: These hazes are due to single yeast cells that don't sink to the bottom of the wine container. There is no reaction to methylated spirits or iodine. The cells can be removed by filtering, or will tend to settle naturally after lengthy maturation.

Lactic acid bacteria hazes: These hazes are revealed by a silky sheen that is seen when the jar of wine is swirled. Sulfating with 150 ppm sulfur dioxide (3 Campden tablets per 5 quarts, 4.5 liters) will clear the wine, although in some cases finings may have to be used.

Re-fermentation hazes: Sometimes a tiny yeast colony reestablishes itself after primary racking and the wine remains cloudy with active yeast cells. If this occurs, you should see a small train of bubbles rising to the surface of the wine and a yeast sediment forming. The wine should be treated with 100 ppm sulfur dioxide (2 Campden tablets per 5 quarts, 4.5 liters), or allowed to complete its fermentation in the normal way if desired.

General notes: Wines that remain cloudy after the above treatments can be cleared either by fining or by filtration. Finings can be purchased from most suppliers and should be used as instructed on the pack. If the finings fail to work, a small amount of grape tannin or tannic acid should be added to the wine (say ¼-½ teaspoon, about 5 milliliters, per 5 quarts, 4.5 liters), as finings only work in the presence of tannin. Such an addition may be necessary after fining to restore the astringency required in a wine (white wines particularly). Filtration should rarely be practiced, as it spoils more wines than it improves.

Chapter 2

SHERRY (DRY AND SWEET)

The soft warmth of sherry has ushered in many romantic evenings and comforted many weary travelers over the highways of life. The excellence of this wine, the Spanish would say, is due to the very fine quality of their grapes and to the techniques employed, particularly that involving the formation of a yeast film, or flor, that gives a unique bouquet and flavor to their dry fino sherries.

Sherry is essentially a fortified white wine produced in a limited area around Jerez de la Frontera, a town in southern Spain between Seville and Cadiz. The predominant soil of the area is a dazzling white earth known as *alberiza*, which contains a high proportion of gypsum, and although vines planted in *alberiza* give smaller yields, the quality of the grapes is considered to be better than those grown in the greater-yielding clay or sandy soils also found in the region.

In Great Britain, a great deal of research has been conducted on sherry production, and indeed it is still being carried out in research laboratories and by individual winemakers. Enough is now known that at-home winemakers can produce sherries that will satisfy all but the out-and-out sherry connoisseur.

It is not the intention to dig deeply into the background information of sherry production, but rather to concentrate this wisdom into carefully constructed recipes and to outline a simple technique that will produce the desired results.

First, it is necessary to give some thought to the selection of suitable ingredients. The illustrious grape has, in normal years, qualities of balance that few other fruits can even approach. Once these qualities are known, however, it is possible to devise combinations of materials that, together, will come close to matching the high standards set by the grape.

Fruits obviously fulfill more of the desired qualities than other ingredients, but not all fruits are suited for the purpose. Red fruits, for example, contain a great deal of tannin, which is not in character with sherry. Again, citrus fruits contain the wrong sort of acid. Such ingredients as yellow plums, greengages, figs, raisins, sultanas (seedless white grapes), and white grape concentrate are very suitable. Their own flavors are often not what are wanted, so that considerable dilution is necessary, which in turn causes a lack of body.

Two principal ingredients can supply body to a wine (other than grains such as wheat or barley, which are not suitable because of their non-vinous flavor). These are bananas and parsnips. It must be mentioned here that beetroots can also supply body and lose their color rapidly, but their earthy flavor tends to persist unless one is prepared to be very patient and mature the wine for a long time.

Gypsum

Another ingredient that plays a part in sherry making is calcium sulfate, better known as gypsum or plaster of Paris. Not only does gypsum form part of the soil of Jerez, it is also scattered over the grapes before pressing. It has the effect of increasing the acidity of the must, but at the same time appears to play a part in sherry flor formation. Some people seem to find it difficult to obtain this chemical, though some suppliers will order it for you if you are willing to purchase 2 pounds (about 1 kilogram) or more. For these people, it must be admitted that a flor can be obtained without gypsum, as our own experiments have proved, but at the same time, the sherry film flourishes much better on a wine in which gypsum has been used than on an ordinary wine.

Alcohol also affects flor growth. It appears that sherry flor yeast can only live in certain alcoholic ranges. If a wine contains about 3 pounds (1.3 kilograms) of sugar per 5 quarts (4.5 liters), including whatever sugar is in the fruit or vegetable used, one achieves the correct amount of alcohol, provided of course that fermentation is complete and almost all the sugar is converted into alcohol. For those who use a hydrometer, the starting gravity range is from 110-120.

In a Spanish bodega, a cellarman tests the clarity of sherry by candlelight.

Once the wine has finished fermenting, it is racked into containers that are only three-quarters filled and the neck of the jar, or bunghole, is plugged with cotton wool, which is renewed occasionally. Then the wine must not be touched in any way until bottling time—no further racking, no movement, no disturbance of any kind.

THE FLOR

It is not difficult to recognize a flor. At first, a few small islands of yeast appear. These gradually become more numerous until the whole surface of the must is covered and the upper surface packs together until it looks like cheese with fine lines drawn across it. Underneath, the yeast hangs down in short stringy lumps that eventually break off, fall to the bottom and autolyze, providing food for the surface yeast and playing a big part in the ultimate flavor of the sherry.

Sherry (dry and sweet)

If a flor is obtained, then the wine is best kept as a dry sherry. If, on the other hand, no flor is obtained, the sherry flavor will still appear to some extent (though not with so smooth a flavor) and the wine is best converted into a sweet sherry.

The following basic method is suitable for making all types of sherry wine.

Basic Method

1. Follow the procedure detailed in the recipe for preparing the must and conducting the fermentation.
2. When the fermentation is complete, siphon off (rack) the wine into a container big enough to allow a fair air space above the wine and plug the container with cotton wool. This racking is the only one in sherry making and it is all-important that pulp debris does not get sucked into the new container. If by any chance this does occur, it is best to do a second racking about two weeks later in order to remove this pulp.
3. Leave the jar in a cool place, 50°-60°F (12°-15°C), and do not disturb it.
4. A flor may form in a few weeks or months. The jar must then be left until the entire flor has finally sunk to the bottom, after which the wine can be bottled.
5. If a flor does not form (as should be the case for sweet oloroso-type sherries) the wine can be sweetened with white grape concentrate or sugar syrup shortly before bottling unless the winemaker prefers to leave it dry. A raisin extract prepared by boiling 1 pound (450 grams) of raisins in 2.5 pints (1.1 liters) of water for half an hour, carefully straining off pulp and evaporating the extract to about half its original volume, can also be used for sweetening.

Original Dry Fino Sherry 1

This recipe demonstrated the possibility of flor formation in Great Britain.

INGREDIENTS

- 1 lb. (450 g.) bananas
- 2 lb. (900 g.) apples
- 1 oz. (30 g.) gypsum
- 1/20 oz. (2 g.) tannic acid
- 1/7 oz. (4 g.) ammonium phosphate (or 1 nutrient tablet)
- Sherry yeast
- 1¼ lb. (560 g.) sugar, boiled in 15 fl. oz. (430 ml.) water and stored for use as detailed in the method
- Water to 5 quarts (4.5 liters)
- 20 fl. oz. (570 ml.) white grape concentrate
- ½ oz. (15 g.) cream of tartar
- ¼ oz. (7½ g.) pectic enzyme

METHOD

Boil bananas, including skins, in 5 pints (2 liters) water for half an hour. Meanwhile, core apples. Chop and place in a polyethylene bucket. Strain liquor from bananas over apples. Add grape concentrate. Cover bucket with blanket and allow to cool. When cool, add cream of tartar, gypsum, pectic enzyme, tannic acid, ammonium phosphate, and yeast starter. Stir twice daily, keeping well covered in between, and after three days, strain off the apples and continue fermentation. Add the remaining sugar syrup from this point on at the rate of 5 fl. oz. (150 ml.) per day until all has been absorbed, then top with water to 5 quarts (4.5 liters). Thereafter, continue from Step 2 in the basic method.

Dry Fino Sherry 2

INGREDIENTS

- 1 lb. (450 g.) parsnips
- 2 lb. (900 g.) apple
- 1 lb. (450 g.) sultanas (seedless white grapes)
- 2 lb. (900 g.) sugar dissolved in 20 fl. oz. (570 ml.) water
- ½ oz. (15 g.) pectic enzyme
- Yeast nutrients
- Sherry yeast starter
- 1 oz. (30 g.) gypsum
- ½ oz. (15 g.) tartaric acid
- ½ oz. (15 g.) cream of tartar
- Water to 5 quarts (4.5 liters)

METHOD

Scrub the parsnips and cut into chunks. Boil the latter in 6.25 pints (3 liters) of water for 10 minutes, and then strain off over raisins and sliced apples in a plastic bucket. Add all the other ingredients except the yeast, pectic enzyme, and 20 fl. oz. (570 ml.) of the sugar syrup (there should be 2.5 pints (1.1 liters) altogether). When cool, add the pectic enzyme and the yeast starter and ferment on the pulp for four days, stirring twice daily. Keep the bucket well covered in the meantime to exclude insects. Strain off the pulp and add 5 fl. oz. (150 ml.) of sugar syrup. Add the rest of the sugar syrup in 5-fl.-oz. (150-ml.) doses every 3 days. If a hydrometer is used, add the sugar syrup whenever a specific gravity of 5 or less is recorded. Once the sugar additions are complete, top off the jar to 5 quarts (4.5 liters) with water and proceed as detailed in the basic method.

Dry Fino Sherry 3

INGREDIENTS

- 4 lb. (1.8 kg.) greengages or yellow plums
- 1 lb. (450 g.) peaches
- ½ lb. (225 g.) sultanas (seedless white grapes) or raisins
- 1½ lb. (675 g.) sugar dissolved in 15 fl. oz. (430 ml.) water
- ½ oz. (15 g.) cream of tartar
- Yeast nutrients
- Sherry yeast starter
- 10 fl. oz. (280 ml.) white grape concentrate
- 1 oz. (30 g.) gypsum
- ¼ oz. (10 g.) pectic enzyme
- Water to 5 quarts (4.5 liters)

METHOD

Wash and pit the greengages and peaches. Scald with 5 pints (2 liters) boiling water in which the ½ oz. (15 g.) cream of tartar has been dissolved. Add the sultanas (seedless white grapes) or raisins, gypsum, yeast nutrient, and 10 fl. oz. (280 ml.) of sugar syrup while the must is still hot. When cool, add the pectic enzyme and yeast starter and ferment on the pulp for 2-3 days. Strain off the pulp at the end of this time and add the grape concentrate. After 7 days, add 5 fl. oz. (150 ml.) of sugar syrup and continue the addition of 5 fl. oz. (150 ml.) of sugar syrup at 3-day intervals until all the syrup has been introduced. These sugar additions are best made every time the specific gravity of the must drops below 5 if a hydrometer is used. Finally, top off to 5 quarts (4.5 liters) with water and proceed as described in the basic method.

Dry Fino Sherry 4
22.5 quarts (20 liters), cask maturing

INGREDIENTS

- 15 lb. (6.5 kg.) beetroot
- 4 lb. (1.8 kg.) dried apricots
- Sherry yeast starter
- 5 pints (2.25 liters) white grape concentrate
- 5 lb. (2.25 kg.) sugar dissolved in 3 pints (1.4 liters) water
- 2 lb. (900 g.) raisins
- 1 oz. (30 g.) pectic enzyme
- 4 oz. (110 g.) gypsum
- 2 oz. (55 g.) cream of tartar
- Water to 22.5 quarts (20 liters)
- Yeast nutrient

METHOD

Cut the beetroot into chunks and boil for half an hour in about 15 quarts (13 liters) of water. Strain liquor over washed apricots and raisins. Dissolve the cream of tartar while the must is still hot and add the gypsum, yeast nutrients, and 20 fl. oz. (570 ml.) of sugar syrup. When cool, add the pectic enzyme and yeast starter and ferment on the pulp for 3-4 days. Strain off the pulp, press lightly, and then add the grape concentrate. After 7-10 days, add 20 fl. oz. (570 ml.) of sugar syrup and continue adding 20 fl. oz. (570 ml.) of sugar syrup every 3 days until it has all been introduced. The winemaker using the hydrometer should follow the usual pattern of adding the 20 fl. oz. (570 ml.) of sugar syrup whenever a specific gravity of 5 or less is recorded. Finally, top off to 22.5 quarts (20 liters) with water and proceed as detailed in the basic method.

Note that this wine should be matured in cask for at least 3 years. Otherwise, it is apt to prove disappointing. Beetroot-based wines are notoriously slow to develop, but are capable of attaining excellent quality given sufficient time.

Dry Fino Sherry 5
22.5 quarts (20 liters), maturing

INGREDIENTS

- 4 lb. (1.8 kg.) bananas
- 9 lb. (4 kg.) parsnips
- 2 lb. (900 g.) raisins or sultanas (seedless white grapes)

- 5 pints (2.25 liters) white grape concentrate
- 2 oz. (55 g.) cream of tartar
- 4 oz. (110 g.) gypsum
- 1½ oz. (45 g.) tartaric acid
- 1 oz. (30 g.) pectic enzyme
- Yeast nutrients
- Sherry yeast starter
- Sugar as required in method
- Water to 22.5 quarts (20 liters)

METHOD

Scrub the parsnips and cut into chunks. Boil in water for 10 minutes and carefully strain off the pulp. Peel the bananas, cut into slices, and boil both skins and fruit in water for half an hour. Again, carefully strain off the pulp. Boil the raisins or sultanas (seedless white grapes) in water for half an hour, strain off the pulp carefully, and boil the pulp with a fresh quantity of water for half an hour. Again, strain off the pulp. Strain the combined banana, parsnip, and raisin extracts again through a fine sieve or straining bag and dissolve the cream of tartar in the hot liquor. Also add the tartaric acid, yeast nutrients, and gypsum at this stage, leaving the gypsum addition until last. Stir the must thoroughly to disperse the gypsum and ensure good mixing. When cool, add the grape concentrate and sufficient sugar syrup and water to give 22.5 quarts (20 liters) of must with an initial gravity of 110-120. Finally, add the pectic enzyme and yeast starter and ferment to dryness. From here, proceed as directed in the basic method.

This wine should preferably be matured in a cask and should be kept for several years before drinking; otherwise it is apt to be disappointing.

Oloroso Sherry 1

22.5 quarts (20 liters), cask maturing

INGREDIENTS

- 20 lb. (9 kg.) apples
- 9 lb. (4 kg.) parsnips
- 4 lb. (1.8 kg.) figs
- 4 lb. (1.8 kg.) bananas
- 8 lb. (3.6 kg.) sugar dissolved in 5 pints (2.25 liters) water
- Water to 22.5 quarts (20 liters)
- 1 oz. (30 g.) tartaric acid
- Yeast nutrients
- Sherry yeast starter
- 5 pints (2.25 liters) white grape concentrate
- 1 oz. (30 g.) pectic enzyme

METHOD

Scrub the parsnips and cut into chunks. Peel and slice the bananas, discarding the skins. Boil the parsnips in water for 10 minutes, and then strain off the pulp. Boil the banana slices in water for half an hour and again strain off the pulp. Wash the figs thoroughly and slice the apples. Pour the banana and parsnip extracts over the apples and figs and add the tartaric acid, yeast nutrients, and 5 pints (2.25 liters) of sugar syrup and adjust the volume to 17.5 quarts (15 liters). When cool, add the pectic enzyme and yeast starter. Ferment on the pulp for 4-5 days, then strain off carefully and add the grape concentrate. After a further 10 days, add 20 fl. oz. (570 ml.) of sugar syrup and repeat the addition every 3 days until all the syrup has been introduced (a hydrometer will considerably assist in judging the best time to add the sugar). Finally, top off to 22.5 quarts (20 liters) with water and proceed as specified in the basic method. Maturation for several years in a cask is advisable.

Sweet Oloroso Sherry 2

INGREDIENTS

- 1 lb. (450 g.) bananas
- 2 lb. (900 g.) raisins
- 1 lb. (450 g.) dried apricots or prunes (or 4 lb. (1.8 kg.) fresh apricots)
- ¼ oz. (10 g.) tartaric acid
- Yeast nutrients
- 2 lb. (900 g.) sugar dissolved in 20 fl. oz. (570 ml.) water
- ¼ oz. (10 g.) pectic enzyme
- Sherry yeast starter
- Water to 5 quarts (4.5 liters)

METHOD

Peel the bananas and cut into slices, discarding the skins. Boil the slices in 6.25 pints (3 liters) of water for half an hour and strain over the other fruit (if fresh apricots are used, remove the pits). Add the tartaric acid and yeast nutrients. When cool, add the yeast and pectic enzyme and ferment on the pulp for 3-4 days. Strain off the pulp at the end of this time and add 20 fl. oz. (570 ml.) sugar syrup. After 7-10 days, add 5 fl. oz. (150 ml.) sugar syrup and repeat the procedure every 3 days until all sugar has been added. Use the hydrometer to control sugar additions in the usual way. Finally, top off to 5 quarts (4.5 liters) and proceed as in the basic method.

Oloroso Sherry 3

INGREDIENTS

- 4 lb. (1.8 kg.) parsnips
- 1 lb. (450 g.) bananas
- 1 lb. (450 g.) raisins
- 20 fl. oz. (570 ml.) white grape concentrate
- ½ oz. (15 g.) tartaric acid
- ¼ oz. (10 g.) pectic enzyme
- Yeast nutrients
- Sherry yeast starter
- 1½ lb. (675 g.) sugar dissolved in 15 fl. oz. (430 ml.) water
- Water to 5 quarts (4.5 liters)

METHOD

Scrub the parsnips and cut into chunks. Peel the bananas and cut into slices. Boil both ingredients together or separately in a total of 5 pints (2.25 liters) of water and strain the hot liquor over the raisins. Add the yeast nutrient, tartaric acid, and 10 fl. oz. (280 ml.) of sugar syrup. When cool, add the pectic enzyme and yeast starter. Ferment on the pulp for 3 days, then strain off the raisins and add the grape concentrate. After 7-10 days, add 5 fl. oz. (150 ml.) sugar syrup and add further doses of 5 fl. oz. (150 ml.) at 3-day intervals until all the sugar has been added. Finally, top off to 5 quarts (4.5 liters) with water and follow the instructions given in the basic method.

Oloroso Sherry 4

Very full-bodied dessert wine

INGREDIENTS

- 2 lb. (900 g.) bananas
- 2 lb. (900 g.) peaches
- 1 lb. (450 g.) figs
- 1 lb. (450 g.) raisins
- 20 fl. oz. (570 ml.) white grape concentrate
- Water to 5 quarts (4.5 liters)
- ¼ oz. (10 g.) pectic enzyme
- Yeast nutrient
- 1½ lb. (675 g.) sugar dissolved in 20 fl. oz. (570 ml.) water
- Sherry yeast starter
- ½ oz. (15 g) tartaric acid

METHOD

Peel and slice the bananas; discard the skins. Boil the slices in 5 pints (2.25 liters) of water for half an hour. Meanwhile, wash the figs and raisins thoroughly to remove dirt and possible sulfite. Cut into halves. Strain the banana liquor over the figs, raisins, and peaches (with pits removed). Add the tartaric acid, yeast nutrients, and 10 fl. oz. (280 ml.) sugar syrup. When cool, add the yeast and pectic enzyme and ferment on the pulp for 2-3 days. Strain off the pulp carefully and add the grape concentrate. After 7-10 days, add 5 fl. oz. (150 ml.) sugar syrup and continue such additions at 3-day intervals until all the sugar has been introduced. The hydrometer may be used to control the sugar additions if desired. Finally, top off to 5 quarts (4.5 liters) with water and proceed as detailed in the basic method.

Full-bodied Oloroso Sherry 5
22.5 quarts (20 liters), cask maturing

INGREDIENTS
- 20 lb. (9 kg.) yellow plums or greengages
- 4 lb. (1.8 kg.) dried apricots
- 6 lb. (2.7 kg.) sugar dissolved in 3.75 pints (1.7 liters) water
- 2.5 pints (1.1 liters) white grape concentrate
- 1 oz. (30 g.) pectic enzyme
- Yeast nutrients
- 4 lb. (1.8 kg.) raisins
- Sherry yeast starter
- Water to 22.5 quarts (20 liters)

METHOD
Remove the pits from the plums or greengages and mix with the apricots and raisins. Scald with 15 quarts (13.5 liters) of boiling water and add the yeast nutrients and 2.5 pints (1.1 liters) sugar syrup. When cool, add the pectic enzyme and yeast starter and ferment on the pulp for 4 days. Strain off the pulp, press lightly, and add the grape concentrate. After 7 days, add 5 fl. oz. (150 ml.) sugar syrup, and repeat the additions every 3 days until all the sugar has been introduced. These sugar additions are, of course, best made with the aid of the hydrometer, the syrup being added at the rate of 5 fl. oz. (150 ml.) per 5 quarts (4.5 liters) of must every time the specific gravity drops below 5. Finally, top off to 22.5 quarts (20 liters) and proceed as in the basic method.

This wine is best matured in cask for several years to allow its great potential to develop.

Chapter 3

PORT

Of all the wines that amateur winemakers produce, a deep rich red wine is more often than not the favorite, and the remark is often heard regarding a choice homemade wine: "It's just like port." In truth, many are not a bit like port, but are just good dessert wines. Nevertheless, a careful analysis of their characteristics would show that had there been a few alterations to their ingredients or to their method of production, they could indeed have become very much like port.

True ports, of course, are made from the grapes of the Douro Valley, in Portugal, and shipped to us from Oporto. Apart from white port, all ports are rich red full-bodied wines, and these characteristics are the main points to have in mind when choosing the ingredients and their quantity to make a port wine. In addition, however, port has a distinctly fruity taste, which sets it apart from many other dessert wines. In the commercial world, this effect is achieved by stopping the fermentation with brandy before more than half the sugar in the must has been transformed into alcohol and carbon dioxide. Because few amateur winemakers will want to use this method, a careful selection of ingredients is needed to keep the fruity flavor. Another method is to mix a mature port-type wine with a younger one, and while the mature wine will impart its maturity to the younger one, the fruitiness of the young wine will tend to come through the blend. A happy evening can be spent tasting and comparing various blends in this way.

The high-alcohol content of port (around 20 percent) is obtained by fortification, but because this is not envisaged in the ordinary way, very great care must be taken to start off with a well-balanced must rich in nutrients, and to ensure sugar syrup is added little by little so the very limit of alcohol production is reached.

It is our impression that port yeast does not reach as high an alcohol tolerance as some other types of yeast, and this seems quite reasonable because, in practice, the yeast is never called upon to produce more than 5-10 percent alcohol before being killed off with brandy. If yeast manufacturers state that their port yeast will, in fact, produce 18 percent alcohol under ideal conditions, then such yeast is suitable for the purpose, but if in doubt, it seems preferable to use a good Madeira yeast, which is certainly

capable of producing this high figure. If Madeira wine was not heat-treated as part of its production, it would end up very much more like port.

The two outstanding port ingredients are undoubtedly elderberries and bilberries, although cherries and blackberries are also very suitable, and sloes, damsons, raspberries, loganberries, and black currants are very useful for imparting the fruitiness required. Red grape concentrate is also useful, though if used on its own, it tends to produce a wine rather like British port-type wines, which are generally made in this manner. Its powerful function is to impart a vinous character to the wine.

The following recipes have been prepared on a graded basis of expense, ranging from inexpensive ones, where fruits are collected from the garden, to one or two recipes of great magnificence. These latter do produce wines of such richness, finesse, and body that they compare favorably with most ports other than those of vintage or tawny quality. Their cost of production is often rather high by amateur-winemaker standards. Still, it is worth making one such brew in a lifetime if only to reminisce about it in the evening of one's life.

In the recipes, quantities of fresh fruit are quoted. Dried fruits can always be used, 1 pound (450 grams) of dried fruits being substituted for every 3 pounds (1.3 kilograms) of fresh fruit.

Similarly, a packet of dried flowers can be used instead of fresh flowers (replacing 10 fl. oz. (280 ml.) of fresh flowers).

Port: Basic Method

1. Prepare the must and commence the fermentation as directed in each recipe.
2. Add the sugar in stages as follows: If a hydrometer is employed, add 5 fl. oz. (150 ml.) sugar syrup per 5 quarts (4.5 liters) every time the specific gravity drops to 5 or less. Continue these sugar additions until fermentation ceases. If no hydrometer is available, the wine must be tasted regularly and the previous 5-fl.-oz. (150-ml.) dose of sugar syrup per 5 quarts (4.5 liters) added whenever the wine tastes as if it contains little sugar. This latter procedure is more hazardous and not advisable in view of the easy control offered by the hydrometer. The sugar syrup is made by dissolving 2 lb. (900 g.) of sugar in 20 fl. oz. (570 ml.) of water at the boil and allowing this solution to cool before use.
3. Rack the wine off its lees within a week of fermentation reaching completion. Add two Campden tablets per 5 quarts (4.5 liters).
4. Rack for a second time as soon as a significant new deposit forms, or after 3 months, whichever comes first.
5. Carry out the third racking as per Step 4 (previous).
6. Rack at about 4-month intervals after the third racking.

7. Persistent hazes still present when the wine is 1-year-old should be removed by fining.

8. Store the wine for at least 12 months, but preferably for 18-24 months Casks are much better than glass for this purpose.

Recipe 1
INGREDIENTS

- 3 lb. (1.3 kg.) elderberries
- 2 lb. (900 g.) bananas
- 20 fl. oz. (570 ml.) red grape concentrate
- ½ lb. (225 g.) raspberries
- 10 fl. oz. (280 ml.) elderflowers
- Yeast nutrients
- Port yeast starter
- Sugar as required
- Water to 5 quarts (4.5 liters)

METHOD

Peel the bananas (discarding the skins) and cut into slices. Boil in 5 pints (2.25 liters) of water for half an hour, and then strain carefully while still hot over the crushed elderberries and raspberries and add the yeast nutrients. When cool, add the yeast starter and ferment on the pulp for not more than 24 hours. Strain off the pulp and press it lightly. Add the elderflowers and grape concentrate to the must and strain off the flowers 3 days later. Finally, continue the fermentation as directed in the basic method. One pound (450 g.) dried elderberries can be used here when fresh ones are not available.

Recipe 2
INGREDIENTS

- 6 lb. (2.7 kg.) damsons
- 1 lb. (450 g.) bananas
- 2 lb. (900 g.) raisins
- 10 fl. oz. (280 ml.) elderflowers
- ¼ oz. (10 g.) pectic enzyme
- Yeast nutrients
- Port yeast starter
- Sugar as required
- Water to 5 quarts (4.5 liters)

METHOD

Wash the raisins and damsons thoroughly and remove the pits from the latter. Peel the bananas (discarding the skins) and cut into slices. Boil the banana slices in 7.5 pints (3 liters) of water for half an hour, and then strain while hot over the damsons and raisins. Add the yeast nutrients. When cool, add the pectic enzyme and yeast starter and ferment on the pulp for 3-4 days. Strain off the pulp and lightly press it. Add the elderflowers and strain off the flowers 3 days later. Proceed as directed in the basic method.

Recipe 3
INGREDIENTS

- 6 lb. (2.7 kg.) cherries
- 1 lb. (450 g.) bananas
- 20 fl. oz. (570 ml.) red grape concentrate
- ½ lb. (225 g.) raspberries
- 10 fl. oz. (280 ml.) elderflowers
- Yeast nutrients
- Port yeast starter
- Sugar as required
- Water to 5 quarts (4.5 liters)
- ¼ oz. (10 g.) pectic enzyme

METHOD
Wash the cherries. Peel the bananas (discarding the skins), cut into slices, and boil in 5 pints (2.25 liters) of water for half an hour. Strain while hot over the cherries and crushed raspberries and add the yeast nutrients. When cool, add the pectic enzyme, grape concentrate, and yeast starter. Ferment on the pulp for 4-5 days, crushing the cherries daily to facilitate color and juice extraction, then strain off carefully. Add the elderflowers, and three days later, strain off the flowers. Finally, proceed as directed in the basic method.

Recipe 4
INGREDIENTS

- 3 lb. (1.3 kg.) sloes
- 1 lb. (450 g.) bananas
- 1 lb. (450 g.) raisins
- 20 fl. oz. (570 ml.) red grape concentrate
- 10 fl. oz. (280 ml.) elderflowers
- Yeast nutrients
- Port yeast starter
- Sugar as required
- Water to 5 quarts (4.5 liters)
- ¼ oz. (10 g.) pectic enzyme

METHOD
Peel the bananas (discarding the skins), cut into slices, and boil in 6.25 pints (3 liters) of water for half an hour. Remove pits from the sloes, if possible, but otherwise crush the fruit and strain the hot banana extract over the sloes and raisins. Add the yeast nutrients. When cool, mix in the grape concentrate, pectic enzyme, and port yeast starter. Ferment on the pulp for 2 days, then strain off and press lightly. Add the elderflowers and strain off again after 3 days. Continue as instructed in the basic method.

Recipe 5
INGREDIENTS

- 6 lb. (2.7 kg.) bilberries
- 1 lb. (450 g.) bananas
- 2 lb. (900 g.) raisins
- 10 fl. oz. (280 ml.) elderflowers
- Yeast nutrients
- Port yeast starter
- Sugar as required
- Water to 5 quarts (4.5 liters)
- ¼ oz. (10 g.) pectic enzyme

METHOD
Peel the bananas (discarding the skins), cut into slices, and boil in 6.25 pints (3 liters) of water for half an hour. Strain while hot over the crushed bilberries and raisins. Add the yeast nutrients. When cool, add the pectic enzyme and yeast starter and ferment on the pulp for 4 days. Strain off the fruit, press lightly, and add the elderflowers. Strain off the flowers after a further 3 days, then follow the instructions detailed in the basic method.

Recipe 6
INGREDIENTS

- 4 lb. (1.8 kg.) red plums
- 2 lb. (900 g.) elderberries
- 20 fl. oz. (570 ml.) red grape concentrate
- 10 fl. oz. (280 ml.) elderflowers
- 1 lb. (450 g.) bananas
- Yeast nutrients
- Port yeast starter
- Sugar as required
- Water to 5 quarts (4.5 liters)
- ¼ oz. (10 g.) pectic enzyme

METHOD

Peel the bananas (discarding the skins), cut into slices, and boil in 5 pints (2.5 liters) of water for half an hour. Strain into a clean plastic bucket. Crush the elderberries and strain off the juice. Add 2.5 pints (1.1 liters) of hot banana extract to the residual elderberry pulp, stir, and strain off again in 5 minutes. Repeat this leaching of the elderberry pulp with the remaining 2.5 pints (1.1 liters) of banana extract. Add the banana and elderberry extract to the washed plums (with pits removed). Add the yeast nutrients. When cool (probably within a few hours in this case), add the pectic enzyme and yeast starter. Ferment on the pulp for 4 days, and then strain off carefully. Add the grape concentrate and elderflowers, straining off the latter after a further 3 days. Proceed as instructed in the basic method.

Recipe 7
INGREDIENTS

- 3 lb. (1.3 kg.) elderberries
- 3 lb. (1.3 kg.) blackberries
- 1 lb. (450 g.) raisins
- 20 fl. oz. (570 ml.) red grape concentrate
- 1 lb. (450 g.) bananas
- 10 fl. oz. (280 ml.) elderflowers
- Yeast nutrients
- Port yeast starter
- Sugar as required
- Water to 5 quarts (4.5 liters)

METHOD

Peel the bananas (discarding the skins), cut into slices, and boil in 5 pints (2.5 liters) of water for half an hour. Strain while hot over the crushed elderberries, blackberries, and raisins and add the yeast nutrients. When cool, add the yeast starter and ferment on the pulp for 24 hours. Strain off and lightly press the pulp. Add the grape concentrate and elderflowers and strain off the latter 3 days later. Continue as instructed in the basic method.

Recipe 8
INGREDIENTS

- 6 lb. (2.7 kg.) blackberries
- 1 lb. (450 g.) bananas
- 2 lb. (900 g.) raisins
- 10 fl. oz. (280 ml.) elderflowers
- Yeast nutrients
- Port yeast starter
- Sugar as required
- Water to 5 quarts (4.5 liters)

METHOD

Peel the bananas (discarding the skins), cut into slices, and boil in 7.5 pints (3 liters) of water for half an hour. Strain over the crushed blackberries and raisins and add the yeast nutrients. When cool, add the yeast starter and ferment on the pulp for 2-3 days. Strain off and press the pulp lightly, then add the elderflowers. Strain off the flowers after an additional 3 days. Finally, proceed as directed in the basic method.

This wine should go tawny within a few months. Make a 22.5-quart (20-liter) quantity of wine by scaling this recipe up approximately so that the wine can then receive the benefits of maturation in the cask.

Recipe 9

To make 22.5 quarts (20 liters)

INGREDIENTS

- 15 lb. (6.5 kg.) elderberries
- 7 lb. (3.1 kg.) bananas
- 4 lb. (1.8 kg.) raisins
- 2.5 pints (1.1 liters) red grape concentrate
- 2.5 pints (1.1 liters) elderflowers
- Yeast nutrients
- Port yeast starter
- Sugar as required
- Water to 22.5 quarts (20 liters)

METHOD

Peel the bananas (discarding the skins), cut into slices, and boil in about 12.5 quarts (12 liters) of water for half an hour. Crush the elderberries and strain off the juice. Strain half of the hot banana extract over the elderberry pulp. Repeat the procedure with the remaining banana extract. Strain the banana and elderberry extracts again to remove as much pulp debris as possible, and then add the raisins and yeast nutrients. When cool, add the elderflowers and yeast starter and ferment on the pulp for 3 days. Strain off the flowers and raisins, add the grape concentrate, and continue as directed in the basic method. Cask maturation will benefit this wine considerably.

Recipe 10

To make 22.5 quarts (20 liters)

INGREDIENTS

- 12 lb. (5.5 kg.) sloes
- 5 lb. (2.2 kg.) elderberries
- 7 lb. (3.1 kg.) bananas
- 5 pints (2.25 liters) red grape concentrate
- 2.5 pints (1.1 liters) elderflowers
- Yeast nutrients
- Port yeast starter
- Sugar as required
- Water to 22.5 quarts (20 liters)

METHOD

Peel the bananas (discarding the skins), cut into slices, and boil in about 12.5 quarts (12 liters) of water for half an hour. Crush the elderberries and strain off the juice. Strain half the hot banana extract over the elderberry pulp, stir for 5 minutes, and again strain off the pulp. Repeat this procedure with the remaining banana extract. Reject the elderberry pulp. Add the elderberry/banana extract to the crushed sloes (preferably with pits removed) and add the yeast nutrients. When cool, add the yeast and ferment on the pulp for 2 days. Strain off and add the grape concentrate and elderflowers. After another 3 days, strain off the flowers. Finally, proceed as directed in the basic method. Cask maturing is again most advisable.

Recipe 11

To make 22.5 quarts (20 liters)

INGREDIENTS

- 30 lb. (13 kg.) cherries
- 7 lb. (3.1 kg.) bananas
- 6 lb. (2.7 kg.) raisins
- 3 lb. (1.3 kg.) raspberries
- 2.5 pints (1.1 liters) elderflowers
- Yeast nutrients
- Port yeast starter
- Sugar as required
- Water to 22.5 quarts (20 liters)
- ½ oz. (15 g.) pectic enzyme

METHOD

Peel the bananas (discarding the skins), cut into slices, and boil in about 12.5 quarts (12 liters) of water for half an hour. Strain over the washed cherries and crushed raspberries and raisins and add the yeast nutrients. When cool, add the pectic enzyme and yeast starter. Ferment on the pulp for 4-5 days, crushing the cherries once or twice daily to break the skins and facilitate color and juice extraction.

Strain off and lightly press the pulp. Add the elderflowers and strain off 3 days later. Continue as instructed in the basic method. Cask maturing is once more recommended for this wine.

Recipe 12

To make 22.5 quarts (20 liters)

INGREDIENTS

- 12 lb. (5.4 kg.) bilberries
- 12 lb. (5.4 kg.) damsons
- 7 lb. (3.1 kg.) bananas
- 4 lb. (1.8 kg.) raisins
- 2.5 pints (1.1 liters) red grape concentrate
- 2.5 pints (1.1 liters) elderflowers
- ½ oz. (15 g.) pectic enzyme
- Yeast nutrients
- Port yeast starter
- Sugar as required
- Water to 22.5 quarts (20 liters)

METHOD

Peel the bananas (discarding the skins), cut into slices, and boil in about 12.5 quarts (12 liters) of water for half an hour. Strain over the crushed bilberries, pitted damsons, and raisins and add the yeast nutrients. When cool, add the pectic enzyme and yeast starter and ferment on the pulp for 3 days. Strain off and lightly press the fruit. Add the grape concentrate and elderflowers and strain off in a further 3 days. Finally, proceed as directed in the basic method. Cask maturing will improve this wine considerably.

Chapter 4

HOCKS, MOSELLES, AND ALSATIAN WINES

There was once a Roman emperor named Probus who became very worried about the idle temptations to which his troops fell victim along the Rhine boundary of the Roman Empire. The chroniclers were very discreet about the nature of the temptations involved, but it can be assumed that drinking wine was not among them, because the solution arrived at by Probus was to employ the troops busily in planting the hillsides of the Rhine valley with grapevines.

Out of this great endeavor has arisen, through the centuries, the superb group of white table wines known as hocks and Moselles. The word superb is a relative description, because by no means do all the wines of Germany (and Alsace) attain this high degree of excellence. Wines containing such appellations as *spatlese, trockenbeerenauslese,* etc., are the product of vintage years when there is plenty of sunshine at the right time in this northern outpost of viticulture. Some of these wines are very expensive and cost a great deal per bottle. Away down the scale are other wines that contain twice the amount of acid normally found in good amateur wines, and these are not always suitable to the palate.

Moselles are very light dry wines, often drunk within a year of making, that have a charming delicate bouquet, are pleasing to the eye with their greenish tinge, and, with their fresh taste and low alcoholic strength, are ideal thirst quenchers when served chilled on a hot summer's day.

Hocks are more full-bodied than Moselles, have more alcohol and flavor, and, when made from late-picked grapes, are luscious enough to serve as a dessert wine.

The wines of Alsace rarely achieve the brilliance of hocks and Moselles, but they are good honest dry white wines, about which it is said that, "every sip becomes a swallow if you do not take care," and one can easily drink a bottle almost without noticing it—until one stands up to go home!

The type of yeast used is extremely important in making wines of any of these three types, but only certain of these yeast types are available to amateur winemakers. The following table outlines those available at the moment, and summarizes the type of wine to which each yeast corresponds:

*Moselle wines	Approximate alcoholic strength	Character of the wine
Zeltinger	7-9%	Very light, dry, and acidic. Slightly sweeter and more full-bodied in very good years, e.g., 1959.
**Bernkasteler		
Hocks		
Niersteiner	9-12%	Medium to full-bodied. Fairly dry, ranging through medium-dry to medium in sweetness. Can be fairly acidic, especially in poorer years.
**Steinberg		
Rudesheim		
**Johannisberger		
Liebfraumilch		
Alsatian wines		
Riesling	10-12%	Fairly light and slightly acidic. Fairly dry but ranging to medium-dry or medium in sweetness.
Sylvaner		
Traminer		
Gewurztraminer		

*Please note that since this book was first written, more options have become available to the home winemaker. Visit your local winemaking supply store for more information.

**Those types marked with a double asterisk are generally recognized as attaining very good quality and rank among the best German wines. Steinberg yeast is one of the most reliable types currently available to amateur winemakers.

In preparing a gospel of perfection, we have suggested the very best strains. If at anytime you find them unobtainable, settle for a hock yeast or a general-purpose white wine yeast.

It is seen that the alcoholic strength is little more than that of double-strength beers, and indeed many of the lighter wines are gulped rather than sipped. It is difficult for many amateur winemakers to restrain themselves from building up the alcohol by adding more and more sugar syrup to the fermenting must, but it must be emphasized that these wines are very light in body and alcohol, and they will lose their character if they are made into high-alcohol types.

Because the yeast plays so important a part in the flavoring of the ultimate wine, it is important not to extract too much flavor from the ingredients, and lengthy pulp fermentation is to be avoided.

We must also emphasize here a matter that is important to all white wine production, and that is the danger of oxidation. If white wines are exposed to too much air at racking time, or if they are matured in small casks, they develop a bouquet somewhat like a sherry bouquet, except the wine does not taste like sherry. This maderization, as it is called, constitutes a spoiled wine. It is extremely common in amateur winemaking circles, and the only way to avoid this danger is to ensure that every racking is carried out as quickly as possible without much splashing, which forces carbon dioxide out of solution and admits air to the wine, and that sulfating is carried out immediately after each racking at 100 ppm (two Campden tablets per 5 quarts, 4.5 liters). If you intend to mature white wine in casks smaller than 45 quarts (40 liters), it is best to varnish the two end panels to cut down the amount of air entering the wine through the pores of the wood.

One additional point, requiring close attention in the production of these wine types, is the need to have a long cool fermentation. These wines do not have the robust flavor of elderberry, parsnip, or raspberry. They are delicate, and the flavors released by the yeast must not be dissipated into the air by a vigorous fermentation. Consequently, a fermenting temperature of 60°-65°F (15°-17°C) is best (or even 55°-60°F, 13°-15°C), even though this may mean a longer fermentation.

Before detailing the basic method and recipes, let us say a word about serving these wines. Some people drink them out of well-chilled hock glasses. They also have a purpose as a long thirst-quenching drink in the summer when served as two-thirds wine, one-third soda water, with ice, in 10-fluid-ounce (280-milliliter) tumblers. With a slice of lemon on top, this is a very attractive drink for a hot summer's day.

Basic Method

1. Process the fruit, etc., and commence fermentation as outlined under each individual recipe.

2. When fermentation is almost complete (specific gravity down to 1.000), carefully rack the wine, without splashing, into fresh jars and sulfate at 100 ppm (two Campden tablets per 5 quarts, 4.5 liters). It is important not to carry over any fruit pulp at this racking, and if by any chance this does occur, it will tend to sink to the bottom of the jar in about 10 days, at which point the wine should be racked again carefully and an additional Campden tablet per 5 quarts (4.5 liters) added (50 ppm). This sulfite will disappear by the next racking.

3. A light yeast sediment should form, and the wine can be safely left on this for 4 months, after which, the wine should again be racked and once more sulfated at 2 Campden tablets per 5 quarts (4.5 liters), or 100 ppm.

4. The wine should then be bottled immediately after this racking and sulfating, and a further few months in the bottle will mature it. These wines improve for up to 2-3 years, but after that will not normally attain further improvement unless of they are of exceptional merit.

Recipe 1 (Hock)
INGREDIENTS

- 4 lb. (1.8 kg.) rhubarb
- 1 lb. (450 g.) raisins
- 10 fl. oz. (280 ml.) white grape concentrate
- 10 fl. oz. (280 ml.) elderflowers
- Nutrients
- 1½ lb. (675 g.) honey (or 1 lb. (450 g.) sugar)
- Steinberg yeast starter
- Water to 5 quarts (4.5 liters)

METHOD

Wash the rhubarb and cut into chunks. Press the chunks and strain the juice carefully to remove suspended pulp debris. If no press is available, the chunks may be crushed, the juice strained off, and the pulp extracted twice with 2.5 pints (1.1 liters) of cold water each time. The combined extracts should then be strained carefully. Add sufficient water to make up the volume to 7.5 pints (3 liters), then add the nutrients, washed raisins, elderflowers, and yeast starter. Ferment on the pulp for 2-3 days, then strain off and press the pulp lightly. Add the grape concentrate and honey (dissolved in 20 fl. oz. (570 ml.) of water) and make up the volume to 5 quarts (4.5 liters). Proceed as directed in the basic method.

Note:
Chalk treatment should not be attempted here. The above procedure, especially pressing, prevents an unduly large amount of oxalic acid from entering the must. Hot extraction procedures must be avoided for this reason.

Recipe 2 (Hock)
INGREDIENTS

- 1 lb. (450 g.) raisins
- 20 fl. oz. (570 ml.) white grape concentrate
- 15 fl. oz. (430 ml.) elderflowers
- 1½ lb. (675 g.) honey (or 1 lb. (450 g.) sugar)
- Nutrients
- Rudesheim yeast starter
- Water to 5 quarts (4.5 liters)
- ½ oz. (15 g.) malic acid

METHOD

Wash the raisins and add to 7.5 pints (3 liters) of water. Add the elderflowers, grape concentrate, malic acid, and nutrients and stir thoroughly to mix the ingredients. Add the yeast starter and ferment on the pulp for 2-3 days. Strain off the pulp and press lightly. Add the honey (dissolved in 20 fl. oz. (570 ml.) of water) and sufficient water to make up the volume to 5 quarts (4.5 liters). Continue as instructed in the basic method.

Recipe 3 (Moselle)
INGREDIENTS

- 4 lb. (1.8 kg.) green gooseberries
- 20 fl. oz. (570 ml.) white grape concentrate
- 15 fl. oz. (430 ml.) elderflowers
- 1 lb. (450 g.) honey
- ½ oz. (15 g.) pectic enzyme
- Nutrients
- Zeltinger yeast starter
- Water to 5 quarts (4.5 liters)

METHOD

Top, tail, and wash the gooseberries. Scald with 7.5 pints (3 liters) of boiling water and add the honey and nutrients. When cool, crush the fruit by hand then add the elderflowers, pectic enzyme, and yeast starter. Ferment on the pulp for 2 days, then strain off and press the pulp lightly. Add the grape concentrate and sufficient water to make the volume up to 5 quarts (4.5 liters). Proceed as instructed in the basic method.

Recipe 4 (Liebfraumilch)
INGREDIENTS

- 4 lb. (1.8 kg.) cooking apples (Bramley)
- 2 lb. (900 g.) dessert apples
- 1 lb. (450 g.) raisins
- 10 fl. oz. (280 ml.) white grape concentrate
- 10 fl. oz. (280 ml.) elderflowers
- 1 lb. (450 g.) sugar (or 1½ lb. (675 g.) honey)
- Nutrients
- Liebfraumilch yeast starter
- Water to 5 quarts (4.5 liters)

METHOD

Wash the apples, cut into slices, and press out the juice. Strain out suspended pulp particles carefully. Add sufficient water to bring the volume up to 7.5 pints (3 liters), and then add the sugar (dissolved in 10 fl. oz. (280 ml.) of water), nutrients, raisins, elderflowers, and yeast starter. Ferment on the pulp for 2-3 days, then strain off the pulp and press lightly. Add the grape concentrate and sufficient water to make the volume up to 5 quarts (4.5 liters). Continue as directed in the basic method.

If no press is available, the apple slices may be scalded with 5 pints (2.25 liters) of boiling water, and the nutrients, raisins, and sugar added. Add the elderflowers and yeast starter when cool and subsequently proceed as above. This method is less satisfactory than that described above, though still worth trying. It is advisable to add ½ oz. (15 g.) pectic enzyme with the elderflowers when employing this method.

Recipe 5 (Moselle)
INGREDIENTS

- 3.75 pints (1.7 liters) dandelion petals
- 20 fl. oz. (570 ml.) white grape concentrate
- 1½ lb. (675 g.) honey
- ⅔ oz. (20 g.) malic acid
- ⅓ oz. (10 g.) tartaric acid
- Nutrients
- Bernkasteler yeast starter
- Water to 5 quarts (4.5 liters)

METHOD

Scald the dandelion petals and honey with 7.5 pints (3 liters) of boiling water. Add the nutrients and malic and tartaric acids. When cool, add the yeast starter. Ferment on the pulp for 2 days, then strain off and press the pulp lightly. Add the grape concentrate and sufficient water to bring the volume up to 5 quarts (4.5 liters). Proceed as directed in the basic method.

Note:
The dandelions should be gathered on a dry sunny day, otherwise contamination with insects and undesirable microorganisms might be encountered. The petals are best separated from the head with scissors—it is a very laborious task by hand!

Recipe 6 (Hock)
INGREDIENTS

- 4 lb. (1.8 kg.) peaches
- 1 lb. (450 g.) raisins
- 10 fl. oz. (280 ml.) white grape concentrate
- 10 fl. oz. (280 ml.) rose petals
- 1 lb. (450 g.) honey (or ¾ lb. (335 g.) sugar)
- Nutrients
- ½ oz. (15 g.) pectic enzyme
- Johannisberger yeast starter
- Water to 5 quarts (4.5 liters)

METHOD

Pit the peaches and press out the juice. Strain out pulp debris carefully. Dilute to 7.5 pints (3 liters) with water and add the nutrients, washed raisins, honey (dissolved in 10 fl. oz. (280 ml.) of water), and pectic enzyme. Finally, add the yeast starter and rose petals and ferment on the pulp for 2 days. Strain off the pulp and press lightly. Add the grape concentrate and sufficient water to make the volume up to 5 quarts (4.5 liters). Proceed as directed in the basic method, but rack for the first time at a specific gravity of 5-10.

Note:
Pulp fermentation of the peaches is permissible, although pressing is preferable. Add the pitted peaches to 5 pints (2.25 liters) of water together with the raisins, etc., and then ferment on the pulp for 2 days exactly as recommended above.

It is also important to note that delicately perfumed rose petals should be used. With strongly scented petals 5 fl. oz. (150 ml.) per 5 quarts (4.5 liters) will suffice.

Recipe 7 (Hock)
INGREDIENTS

- 1½ lb. (675 g.) gooseberries
- ½ lb. (225 g.) raisins
- 20 fl. oz. (570 ml.) white grape concentrate
- ⅔ oz. (20 g.) malic acid
- 1 lb. (450 g.) honey (or ¾ lb. (335 g.) sugar)
- Nutrients
- Niersteiner yeast starter
- Water to 5 quarts (4.5 liters)

METHOD

Scald the crushed gooseberries and raisins with 7.5 pints (3 liters) of boiling water. Add the nutrients, honey, and malic acid. When cool, add the yeast starter. Ferment on the pulp for 1-2 days, then strain off and press the pulp lightly. Add the grape concentrate and sufficient water to bring the volume up to 5 quarts (4.5 liters). Proceed as instructed in the basic method.

Recipe 8 (Hock)
INGREDIENTS

- 1 lb. (450 g.) white currants
- 2.5 pints (1.1 liters) orange juice
- 20 fl. oz. (570 ml.) white grape concentrate
- 1½ lb. (675 g.) honey
- Nutrients
- Steinberg yeast starter
- Water to 5 quarts (4.5 liters)

METHOD

Juice a sufficient amount of oranges to provide 2.5 pints (1.1 liters) of juice. Strain carefully to remove suspended pulp particles and add to the crushed white currants. Add 5 pints (2.25 liters) of water, the nutrients, and honey (dissolved in 15 fl. oz. (430 ml.) of water). Add the yeast starter and ferment on the pulp for 2 days. Strain off the pulp and press lightly. Add the grape concentrate and sufficient water to bring the volume up to 5 quarts (4.5 liters). Proceed as directed in the basic method, racking for the first time at a specific gravity of 5.

Recipe 9 (Hock)

22.5 quarts (20 liters), short cask maturation (3-6 months)

INGREDIENTS

- 18 lb. (7.8 kg.) rhubarb
- 5 pints (2.25 liters) white grape concentrate
- 2.5 pints (1.1 liters) rose petals
- 5 lb. (2.25 kg.) honey
- Nutrients
- Steinberg yeast starter
- Water to 22.5 quarts (20 liters)

METHOD

Wash the rhubarb and cut into chunks. Press the chunks and strain the juice carefully to remove suspended pulp particles. If no press is available, the rhubarb may be crushed and the juice strained off. The pulp may then be extracted twice with 7.5 quarts (6.75 liters) of cold water each time and the combined juice and extracts strained carefully as above. Add the grape concentrate, nutrients, honey (dissolved in 6.25 pints (2.75 liters) of water), and rose petals. Make up the volume to 22.5 quarts (20 liters) and ferment on the pulp for 2 days. Strain off the pulp and make up the volume to 22.5 quarts (20 liters) with water. Proceed as directed in the basic method, but rack for the first time at a specific gravity of about 8.

Note:
The rhubarb juice should not be treated with chalk for the reasons mentioned in an earlier recipe.

Recipe 10 (Alsatian wine)

22.5 quarts (20 liters), mature in the cask for 3 months

INGREDIENTS

- 18 lb. (7.8 kg.) green gooseberries
- 4 lb. (1.8 kg.) raisins
- 2.5 pints (1.1 liters) white grape concentrate
- 3.75 pints (1.7 liters) elderflower
- 1 oz. (30 g.) pectic enzyme
- 4 lb. (1.8 kg.) sugar
- Nutrients
- Traminer yeast starter
- Water to 22.5 quarts (20 liters)

METHOD

Wash the gooseberries and raisins and scald with 15 quarts (13.5 liters) of boiling water. Add the nutrients and sugar and stir until dissolved. When cool, crush the fruit by hand, and then add the pectic enzyme, elderflower, and yeast starter. Ferment on the pulp for 2 days, then strain off and press the pulp lightly. Add the grape concentrate and make the volume up to 22.5 quarts (20 liters) with water. Continue as instructed in the basic method.

Chapter 5

DRY RED WINES OF FRANCE

The varieties of dry red wines are so numerous that only a general classification is possible.

From the great vintages of Bordeaux (claret) and the mighty Burgundies, to wines from remote villages in South America, red wine is perhaps the most widely consumed wine in the world, and the mainstay of those areas where water is used only for washing.

It might be as well to mention Algerian wines first, because their production totals many millions of gallons each year. These wines are commonly used for blending with the mediocre and nameless wines of Bordeaux, Burgundy, and, specially, the Midi, to provide the *vin ordinaire* that is the staple wine of the French working class. Very little of the blended wine is exported, but enormous quantities are consumed in France—it is the bread-and-butter wine of the shippers.

Some cheap Algerian wine is also used by less scrupulous shippers to stretch the better, but less plentiful, Burgundies, thereby increasing profits. This is a highly reprehensible practice possible with Burgundies, because the many small vineyards sell their wines directly to the shippers for blending with other wines from the district. It is then all too easy to slip in a little Algerian wine. Claret is rarely adulterated in this way, as the vineyard holdings are much larger and the good-quality wines are rarely blended. The climate in Algeria is such that the vine grows well and crops are enormous so that, in consequence, quality tends to suffer.

Many of the better amateur red wines taste rather like Algerian wine, and this is no stigma, for it is an achievement to produce a dry red wine that tastes like a grape wine from ingredients such as elderberries and raisins.

Beaujolais

Beaujolais is the second wine that commands our attention, for we have found by experiment and from judging that when an amateur winemaker produces a really outstanding dry red wine, it seems to be more often like a Beaujolais than any other dry red wine. Beaujolais can be bought by the glass in most bars, and it is worth trying a few glasses to get the taste of it before trying to produce a wine of this type. Beaujolais comes from the most southerly and largest of the Burgundy-wine-producing areas, and it is a good average-quality light red wine that matures early. The Burgundians have a vast rivalry with their claret-producing neighbors in Bordeaux, and they say in their confident superiority that Burgundy does not leave your mouth feeling like the bottom of a parrot's cage, a scornful reference to the practice in Bordeaux of putting young wines in new oak casks, which causes additional tannin to be released into the wine from the oak. They also have a saying in the Beaujolais region that every sip becomes a swallow and every swallow a guzzle, after which, presumably you lie in the sun and sleep it off. Undoubtedly, Beaujolais has become a very popular wine and it is perhaps the easiest of the dry red wines to simulate, often being ready to drink after 1-2 years.

The great majority of true Burgundies, other than Beaujolais, come from the Côte de Nuits and Côte de Beaune. One thing that should warm the hearts of amateur winemakers to this region of France is the fact that the whole area is split up into tiny vineyards, so there are more than 20,000 vineyard owners. Most of these owners work elsewhere during the week, tending their minute vineyards in the evenings and on weekends, rather as the English do their allotments. The annual production of wine from one of these vineyards is often less than that of the avid amateur winemaker. The owners may, in many ways, be regarded as amateur winemakers at heart, who make wine for the sheer love of it and just happen to sell part of their production by chance, as it were, the tiny parcels of wine being handled by cooperatives.

Bordeaux

Let us now take a closer look at Bordeaux, where the red wines known collectively as claret are produced. Bordeaux can well afford to shrug off its disclaimers, for the leading connoisseurs over many centuries have affirmed, and no doubt will for centuries to come, that claret is the absolute monarch of all dry red wines. Even Burgundy pales beside it, provided one has drunk enough to obtain a palate. It is an unfortunate occurrence that more often than not, one's first encounter with claret is at a firm's annual dinner, where, after having had a few gins or whiskies at the reception before the dinner, everyone moves into the dining hall and comes face to face with claret, served with the meal, generally an inferior claret. Under these conditions, the claret tastes like vinegar and one forms the impression that claret is not a wine with which to make closer acquaintance.

For those who have suffered this fate, and their number is surprisingly high, it is better to drink Burgundy, and if you drink enough, you will in time graduate to claret as naturally as summer follows spring. One's palate becomes steadily drier the more wine one drinks, and clarets are on the whole drier than Burgundy, while possessing in addition a greater finesse that only earnest drinking will make apparent.

The best clarets are those that, at the outset, contain too much tannin (like an elderberry wine made with 6 pounds (2.7 kilograms) berries to 5 quarts (4.5 liters). At a year old, such a wine is harsh and almost undrinkable, but because clarets are kept in casks for 2-3 years (and sometimes up to 5 years), and in bottles for another 2-20 years, they assume a quality at the end of this time not possible in wines with less tannin, which mature earlier.

Claret = Goal

Claret is then the absolute goal toward which the amateur winemaker strives in his winemaking, because claret is the best of the dry red wines, and dry red wines are the hardest types of wine to successfully produce. To achieve this goal is difficult, but it can in fact be done. The secret is first to obtain a well-balanced must and secondly to allow proper maturation, preferably in a cask.

In order to approach the desired goal, the must has to conform to certain basic essentials, i.e.:

1. A deep red fruit must be used, and for this purpose elderberries, bilberries, deep red plums, damsons, cherries, sloes, and chokecherries are suitable, whereas blackberries are not, because their color fades with time.

2. A second ingredient is required to provide vinous quality. This can be red grape concentrate, raisins, or sultanas (seedless white grapes). It is not advisable to try to make good dry red wines from red grape concentrate alone, because the resultant wine appears to lack character.

3. The must should be rich in tannin, richer for claret than Burgundy wines, so the wine will prove too harsh for drinking after 6 months.

4. An average acidity of 3.3-4.3 ppt (in terms of sulfuric acid) is desirable, with 3.8 ppt offering a good average value.

5. It should have an alcoholic content of about 10-13 percent (equivalent to a starting gravity of 75-100).

6. A good red wine yeast should be used, such as Pommard, Burgundy, or Bordeaux.

In the following recipes, these factors have been taken care of automatically, and it is only necessary to point out that one cannot be sure whether one's intended claret will turn out more like a Beaujolais or vice versa, so if one is going to name one's wine in this fashion, it is better to wait until bottling time before christening it. Where we have indicated a recipe as a claret (Recipes 3 and 6), its tannin content is higher than that of Burgundy recipes, so adequate maturing will be needed. If the winemaker cannot afford to wait 2 years for maturing, it is better to stick to the Burgundy and Beaujolais recipes.

Basic Method

It should be noted that all recipes are quoted for 22.5-quart (20-liter) quantities. This is a normal cask size used by amateur winemakers in Britain, and is really the minimum size capable of producing top-quality dry red wines. The quantities of ingredients can of course be scaled up or down for larger or smaller volumes of wine. The main essential is that cask maturing should be practiced with red wines where possible.

1. Proceed as indicated in each recipe for processing ingredients and commencing fermentation.

2. When the fermentation has proceeded to dryness, carefully rack the wine into a fresh container. This first racking may be into a glass jar, where it can easily be discerned, after a week or so, whether the wine is clear of pulp debris. If any large amount of such deposit is apparent, rack once more into a cask, this time sulfating with 50 ppm (one Campden tablet per 5 quarts (4.5 liters).

3. Successive rackings should be made at 4-month intervals for at least 1 year, and preferably 2 years. At each racking, the wine should be tasted. During the early rackings, it should appear rather harsh and undrinkable, but with a certain vinous character. Gradually, it should be possible to perceive an element of smoothness creeping in and a disappearance of the harsh initial character.

4. When the wine appears almost drinkable, it should be bottled and the bottles stored for an additional 6 months at least.

5. If one intends to enter these wines in competitions, it is worthwhile to bottle part of the wine in screw-top quart (liter) beer or cider bottles. In this way, any deposit or crust that may form, quite common with red wines, will settle at the bottom and an ordinary wine bottle can be filled from the beer bottle without this sediment being siphoned over with the wine.

Recipe 1
INGREDIENTS
- 10 lb. (4.5 kg.) elderberries
- 10 lb. (4.5 kg.) raisins
- 4 lb. (1.8 kg.) sugar
- Nutrients
- Beaujolais yeast starter
- Water to 22.5 quarts (20 liters)

Dry Red Wines of France

METHOD

Crush the elderberries and strain off the juice. Leach the pulp by adding 5 quarts (4.5 liters) of boiling water, stirring for 5 minutes, and then straining off the pulp. Repeat this treatment with another 5 quarts (4.5 liters) of boiling water. Add the raisins and nutrients to this elderberry extract, followed by another 7.5 quarts (6 liters) of water. When cool, add the yeast starter and ferment on the raisin pulp for 4 days. Strain off the pulp and press lightly. Add the sugar, stir until completely dissolved, and make up the volume to 22.5 quarts (20 liters) with water. Continue as directed in the basic method.

Recipe 2
INGREDIENTS

- 20 lb. (9 kg.) cherries
- 4 lb. (1.8 kg.) raisins
- 2.5 pints (1.1 liters) red grape concentrate
- 4 lb. (1.8 kg.) sugar
- Nutrients
- Pommard yeast starter
- Water to 22.5 quarts (20 liters)

METHOD

Add 17.5 quarts (15 liters) of boiling water to the washed cherries and raisins. Add the nutrients and sugar and stir until dissolved. When cool, add the yeast starter. Ferment on the pulp until a sample drawn off from the bulk is sufficiently deep in color. Strain off and press the pulp lightly. Add the grape concentrate and make the volume up to 22.5 quarts (20 liters) with water. Proceed as instructed in the basic method.

Recipe 3 (Claret)
INGREDIENTS

- 12 lb. (5.4 kg.) elderberries
- 5 lb. (2.2 kg.) greengages
- 2.5 pints (1.1 liters) red grape concentrate
- 6 lb. (2.7 kg.) sugar
- Nutrients
- Bordeaux yeast starter
- Water to 22.5 quarts (20 liters)

METHOD

Crush the elderberries and strain off the juice. Leach the pulp by adding 5 quarts (4.5 liters) of boiling water, stirring for 5 minutes, and then straining off the pulp. Repeat this procedure with another 5 quarts (4.5 liters) of boiling water. Add the pitted greengages, sugar, nutrients, and 5 quarts (4.5 liters) of water to this elderberry extract and stir well until dissolved. When cool, add the yeast starter. Ferment on the pulp for 4 days, then strain off the pulp and press lightly. Add the grape concentrate and make the volume up to 22.5 quarts (20 liters) with water. Proceed as instructed in the basic method.

Recipe 4
INGREDIENTS

- 12 lb. (5.4 kg.) bilberries
- 10 lb. (4.5 kg.) peaches
- 2.5 pints (1.1 liters) red grape concentrate
- 6 lb. (2.7 kg.) sugar
- Nutrients
- Burgundy yeast starter
- Water to 22.5 quarts (20 liters)

METHOD

Crush the bilberries and add the pitted peaches. Add 12.5 quarts (10 liters) of boiling water, sugar, and nutrients and stir until dissolved. When cool, add the yeast starter. Ferment on the pulp until a satisfactory depth of color is attained, then strain off the pulp and press lightly. Add the grape concentrate and sufficient water to make the volume up to 22.5 quarts (20 liters). Proceed as instructed in the basic method.

Recipe 5
INGREDIENTS

- 25 lb. (11 kg.) dessert apples
- 12 lb. (5.4 kg.) elderberries
- 2.5 pints (1.1 liters) red grape concentrate
- 5 lb. (2.25 kg.) sugar
- Nutrients
- Pommard yeast starter
- Water to 22.5 quarts (20 liters)

METHOD

Crush the elderberries and strain off the juice. Add 5 quarts (4.5 liters) of boiling water to the pulp, stir for 5 minutes, and then strain off the pulp. Repeat this treatment with another 5 quarts (4.5 liters) of boiling water. Add the elderberry juice and hot extracts to the washed sliced apples. Dissolve the sugar and nutrients in this solution. When cool, add the yeast starter. Ferment on the pulp for 7 days, then strain off the pulp and press lightly. Add the grape concentrate and sufficient water to make the volume up to 22.5 quarts (20 liters). Proceed as directed in the basic method.

Recipe 6 (Claret)
INGREDIENTS

- 12 lb. (5.4 kg.) sloes or damsons
- 4 lb. (1.8 kg.) raisins
- 5 pints (2.25 liters) red grape concentrate
- 4 lb. (1.8 kg.) honey
- Nutrients
- Bordeaux yeast starter
- Water to 22.5 quarts (20 liters)

METHOD

Wash and crush the sloes and mix with the raisins. (Pit the sloes if possible). Add the honey, nutrients, and 15 quarts (13.5 liters) of boiling water. When cool, add the yeast starter and ferment on the pulp for 2-3 days. Strain off the pulp and press lightly. Add the grape concentrate and sufficient water to bring the volume up to 22.5 quarts (20 liters). Continue as instructed in the basic method. This wine will require a long maturation and is best not attempted unless cask maturing is contemplated.

Dry Red Wines of France

Recipe 7
INGREDIENTS

- 25 lb. (11 kg.) plums (red or blue)
- 4 lb. (1.8 kg.) raisins
- 5 pints (2.25 liters) red grape concentrate
- 2 lb. (900 g.) honey
- Nutrients
- Pommard yeast starter
- Water to 22.5 quarts (20 liters)
- 1 oz. (30 g.) pectic enzyme

METHOD

Wash and pit the plums and add the raisins and honey. Add 15 quarts (13.5 liters) of boiling water and the nutrients. When cool, add the pectic enzyme and yeast starter. Ferment on the pulp for 5-6 days, and then strain off the pulp and press lightly. Add the red grape concentrate and sufficient water to make the volume up to 22.5 quarts (20 liters). Proceed as directed in the basic method.

Chapter 6

WHITE WINES OF FRANCE

During one of the many wars England waged against France, an English general is purported to have said he found the greatest difficulty in working up the proper feeling of hostility, because whenever he thought of wine, he immediately thought of France, and whenever he thought of France, he remembered her rich vineyards. To destroy those vineyards was to him a monstrous sin.

Doubtless another who preferred port replaced the general, but the French vineyards remain, despite wars and other calamities, and from their verdant richness pours forth each year a refreshing river of wine greater in volume than that of any other country in the world.

A great deal of this wine is red, of course, but of the many white wines produced, there are three main types meriting closer attention that can be simulated by the amateur winemaker who realizes the basic characteristics of each type.

Three Whites

These three main types are white Burgundy, Graves, and Sauternes. It should be mentioned, however, that there are many other excellent white-wine-producing areas of France that we have omitted solely because they are as yet not sufficiently well known. White Burgundies are made from grapes that are fully ripened, but not over-ripened. Because all of the sugar is converted to alcohol during fermentation, a dry full-bodied velvety wine results.

MONTRACHET

The great name in white Burgundies is Montrachet, a name familiar to anyone who has travelled to the Riviera down the famous Route Nationale 6 as it passes through part of the Côte d'Or near Chagny. Many wines from adjacent vineyards in the same area trade on the fame of Montrachet by attaching its name to their own, e.g., Puligny-Montrachet. These are all fine wines, but the very best, labeled simply, Le Montrachet, is so rare that only a small quantity of the wine reaches other areas of the world each year (at a high cost per bottle).

POUILLY-FUISSÉ

Pouilly-Fuissé is also well known, and is frequently served chilled with seafood. At its best, it is a superb but short-lived wine, which accounts for the sale prices often quoted for it in wine stores after it is five years old, a good indication of its approaching senility.

CHABLIS

Chablis is perhaps the best-known white Burgundy. Chablis has a certain crispness with a slight acidity, the color is golden with a tinge of green, and it has a sort of gunmetal aftertaste arising from the flinty soil that distinguishes it from other white wines.

Because comparatively little white Burgundy is usually produced, its price is often high in comparison with other white wines. One inexpensive white Burgundy can be found, however, and that is Macon Blanc.

An interesting fact emerges here. In our search for ingredients that will make satisfactory substitutes for the grape, the obvious sometimes escapes us. In one issue of the now out of print magazine *Amateur Winemaker,* there was an article on the use of apricot pulp as one of the best ingredients for a beginner. We were drinking some 8-month-old wine (made according to the recommended recipe) in the office one day when someone said, "Let's go round to the Golden Eagle for a drink." While the ladies of the office went over to gin and bitter lemon, one of the authors asked for white wine and was given the Macon Blanc. It was astonishing to find the apricot and the Macon Blanc were identical in flavor, and the Macon only scored in the matter of bouquet, which can easily be remedied by the inclusion of flowers, e.g., elderflowers. It is worth trying that recipe, for Macon Blanc is one of the best cheap white wines available.

Fruits such as green gooseberries, apricots, or oranges are eminently suitable for producing Chablis-type wines, but generally some white grape concentrate or sultanas (seedless white grapes) are needed in addition in order to obtain the true vinosity. A good Chablis yeast is required, and to obtain the best results from this yeast, great care must be taken both to avoid long pulp fermentations and to preserve the delicate flavor by careful racking. All too many winemakers rack their wines with a great deal of splashing, which forces the bouquet out of the wine and/or causes too much oxidization, and insist on obtaining the last possible drop of wine from the fermenting jar. This often results in pulp being sucked over into the new jar, where it can quietly disintegrate, producing appalling off flavors. Rather than make 5 quarts (4.5 liters) of wine, it is better to make 11.25 pints (5 liters), so a clear 5 quarts (4.5 liters) can be racked off unhindered by pulp debris.

GRAVES

Graves is a Bordeaux wine, and the best Graves are in fact red wines, but the white Graves appeal greatly to many palates, so they are perhaps almost better known than the red wines of this region. Graves is somewhat sweeter than Chablis, and is lower in its acid content. The cheaper wines of this region are sold as Bordeaux Blanc and Bordeaux Supérieur, but these are rarely of much account. You can experiment by purchasing a bottle of cheap Bordeaux Blanc and comparing it with a good amateur white wine. Except perhaps in the matter of bouquet, which is one of the present weaknesses of amateur winemaking, the commercial product will be found to be inferior to the amateur wine.

The fruits mentioned for simulating Chablis can also be used for Graves, though because Graves has a little more body, slightly greater quantities can be used, and in addition, small quantities of bananas can be used with advantage. Greengages and yellow plums are also good ingredients for white-Bordeaux-type wines. A good Bordeaux yeast is required, and the same observations concerning racking will again apply.

SAUTERNES

Sauternes also comes from the Bordeaux region, but differs from other white wines so much that the Sauternes region is always considered distinct from the rest of Bordeaux.

The peculiarity about Sauternes arises from the practice of subjecting the grapes on the vine to the attack of a mold known variously as *Botrytis cinerea*, Noble Rot, or *La Pourriture Noble*. This mold, under the right climatic conditions, causes the grapes to lose some of their water content, so that both sugar and acid increase. In addition, some glycerol (glycerin) is found in the grapes, and several other small chemical changes can be observed. The resultant wine is a sweet or very sweet golden dessert wine of overpowering fragrance with a silkiness and rich flavor that endears itself to connoisseurs as the world's best sweet white wine.

The best Sauternes are superb, culminating in the incomparable Chateau d'Yquem, and it would be misleading the reader to suggest anything approaching these can be fashioned out of the ingredients available to us. Nevertheless, the less-expensive types of Sauternes are fairly easy to simulate, providing the initial must is carefully prepared.

A blend of materials is, of course, required. The basic pattern consists of a light-colored basic ingredient to which grape concentrate, raisins, or sultanas (seedless white grapes) are added for vinosity. The considerable body and fragrance of Sauternes are best obtained by the addition of bananas and flowers respectively. Small amounts of glycerin can also be added as part of the final sweetening procedure prior to bottling, and this will add the silkiness inherent in Sauternes.

CASK WARNING

We would like to issue a slight warning at this point on the use of casks. Amateur winemakers tend to use rather small cooperage, 15-22.5 quart (13.5-20 liter) casks. Unless these are of very close-grained oak, they are *not* suitable for maturing white wines except Sauternes, even with the protection of considerable amounts of sulfite. Too often, too much air gets to the wine, resulting in an oxidized bouquet and taste. It is better to use polypins and demijohns and to rack the wine at 4-month intervals with sulfite additions, unless 45-quart (42.5-liter), or larger, casks are employed.

In the following recipes, the peculiarities of each wine type have been allowed for, but the winemaker will in time realize the principles behind the recipes and be able to design similar recipes for other ingredients he may find suitable. There are many other exciting and interesting wines from France, such as those of the Loire Valley, and the winemaker should undertake the fascinating study of these types whenever an opportunity occurs at wine tastings and the like. The more one knows about the taste and bouquet of commercial wines, the greater will be one's ability to make good wine. We are not trying blindly to imitate commercial wines, but to produce wines of a generally similar nature that will fulfill the same purpose.

Basic Method

1. Process the ingredients as indicated in each recipe.

2. Ferment the wine to dryness, except when making Sauternes-type wines, where the sugar additions may be continued (in doses at a rate of ¼ pound (110 grams) per 5 quarts (4.5 liters.) or in doses of 5 fluid ounces (150 milliliters) of sugar syrup) until a sweet wine results.

3. When fermentation is finished, rack the wine off the lees into glass containers, sulfate with 100 ppm sulfur dioxide (two Campden tablets per 5 quarts, 4.5 liters), and seal with a cork plus fermentation lock, or a cork heavily plugged with cotton wool.

4. Store the wine in a cool place for 4 months, after which time it should be racked again and sulfated as before. In the event of a heavy deposit forming, which might seem to be pulp debris, rack earlier (even as close as two weeks after the first racking) and add one additional Campden tablet per 5 quarts (4.5 liters).

5. Further rackings can be made at 4-month intervals, and care should be taken to see that the jars are topped up at each racking with wine or water.

6. The wine should first become drinkable at about 6 months, but will be at its best in 1-2 years, after which, it will hold its quality for a year or so and then gradually decline. Sauternes-type wines may, however, take slightly longer to mature and will certainly retain their quality for several more years before falling into senility.

Chablis

INGREDIENTS

- 4 lb. (1.8 kg.) green gooseberries
- 20 fl. oz. (570 ml.) white grape concentrate
- 10 fl. oz. (280 ml.) elderflowers
- Water to 5 quarts (4.5 liters)
- 1 lb. (450 g.) sugar
- ½ oz. (15 g.) pectic enzyme
- Nutrients
- Chablis yeast starter

METHOD

Wash, top, and tail the gooseberries. Add the sugar and nutrients to the fruit and add 7.5 pints (4 liters) boiling water. When cool, add the elderflowers, pectic enzyme, and yeast starter. Ferment on the pulp for 3 days, crushing the fruit by hand daily, then strain off the pulp and press lightly. Add the grape concentrate and sufficient water to make up the volume to 5 quarts (4.5 liters). Proceed as directed in the basic method.

White Burgundy (1)

INGREDIENTS

- 2.5 pints (1.1 liters) sweet orange juice
- 20 fl. oz. (570 ml.) white grape concentrate
- 10 fl. oz. (280 ml.) elderflowers
- 1½ lb. (675 g.) honey
- Nutrients
- Burgundy yeast starter
- Water to 5 quarts (4.5 liters)

METHOD

Extract the juice from a sufficient amount of oranges to get 2.5 pints (1.1 liters) of juice. Add the grape concentrate, 2.5 pints (1.1 liters) water, nutrients, elderflowers, and honey and stir until dissolved. Make up to 9 pints (4 liters) with water and add the yeast starter. Ferment on the pulp for 3 days, and then strain off the pulp and make the volume up to 5 quarts (4.5 liters) with water. Continue as instructed in the basic method.

White Burgundy (2)

INGREDIENTS

- 4 lb. (1.8 kg.) apricots
- 1 lb. (450 g.) sultanas (seedless white grapes)
- 10 fl. oz. (280 ml.) yellow rose petals
- 1½ lb. (675 g.) honey
- ½ oz. (15 g.) pectic enzyme
- Nutrients
- Burgundy yeast starter
- Water to 5 quarts (4.5 liters)

METHOD

Wash and pit the apricots and chop up the sultanas (seedless white grapes). Add the nutrients and honey and add 7.5 pints (4 liters) boiling water. When cool, add the rose petals, pectic enzyme, and yeast starter. Ferment on the pulp for 2-3 days, and then strain off the pulp and press lightly. Make up the volume to 5 quarts (4.5 liters) with water and proceed as directed in the basic method.

White Burgundy (3)

INGREDIENTS

- 10 lb. (4.5 kg.) green gooseberries
- 7.5 pints (4 liters) orange juice
- 5 pints (2.25 liters) white grape concentrate
- 2.5 pints (1.1 liters) yellow rose petals
- 5 lb. (2.25 kg.) sugar
- 1 oz. (30 g.) pectic enzyme
- Nutrients
- Burgundy yeast starter
- Water to 22.5 quarts (20 liters)

METHOD

Wash the gooseberries, top and tail and add the nutrients and sugar. Express the juice from a sufficient amount of oranges (about 40 oranges) to give 7.5 pints (4 liters) of juice and add to the gooseberries. Add 12.5 quarts (10 liters) of boiling water and stir until the sugar, etc., has dissolved. When cool, crush the gooseberries (by hand) and add the pectic enzyme, rose petals, and yeast starter. Ferment on the pulp for 3 days, then strain off the pulp and press lightly. Add the grape concentrate and make the volume up to 22.5 quarts (20 liters) with water. Continue as directed in the basic method.

Sauternes (1)

INGREDIENTS

- 6 lb. (2.7 kg.) yellow plums
- 2 lb. (900 g.) bananas
- 20 fl. oz. (570 ml.) white grape concentrate
- 10 fl. oz. (280 ml.) yellow rose petals
- ½ oz. (15 g.) tartaric acid
- ½ oz. (15 g.) malic acid
- 1½ fl. oz. (45 ml.) glycerol
- 1½ lb. (675 g.) sugar
- Nutrients
- Sauternes yeast starter
- Water to 5 quarts (4.5 liters)

METHOD

Peel the bananas (discarding the skins) and cut into slices. Boil the slices in 6.25 pints (3.5 liters) of water for half an hour, and then strain carefully over the pitted plums. Add the acids and nutrients while still hot and dissolve the sugar in the hot liquor. When cool, add the rose petals and yeast starter. Ferment on the pulp for 3-4 days, and then strain off the pulp and press lightly. Add the grape concentrate and glycerol, dilute to 5 quarts (4.5 liters) with water, and proceed as directed in the basic method.

Sauternes (2)

INGREDIENTS

- 4 lb. (1.8 kg.) parsnips
- 2 lb. (900 g.) bananas
- 20 fl. oz. (570 ml.) white grape concentrate
- 20 fl. oz. (570 ml.) elderflowers
- ½ oz. (15 g.) tartaric acid
- ½ oz. (15 g.) malic acid
- 1½ fl. oz. (45 ml.) glycerol
- 1½ lb. (675 g.) sugar
- Nutrients
- Sauternes yeast starter
- Water to 5 quarts (4.5 liters)
- ½ oz. (15 g.) pectic enzyme

METHOD

Peel the bananas (discarding the skins) and cut into slices. Boil the slices together with the washed sliced parsnips in 7.5 quarts (3 liters) of water for half an hour. Strain off carefully and add the nutrients, acids, and glycerol to the hot liquor. When cool, add the elderflowers, pectic enzyme, white grape concentrate, and yeast starter. Ferment on the pulp for 2 days, then strain off the latter. Add the sugar dissolved in a sufficient amount of water to make the volume of the must up to 5 quarts (4.5 liters). Continue as directed in the basic method.

Sauternes (3)

INGREDIENTS

- 20 lb. (9 kg.) peaches
- 10 lb. (4.5 kg.) bananas
- 5 pints (2.25 liters) white grape concentrate
- 2.5 pints (1.1 liters) yellow rose petals
- ¾ oz. (25 g.) tartaric acid
- 6 fl. oz. (180 ml.) glycerol
- 6 lb. (2.7 kg.) honey
- ½ oz. (15 g.) malic acid
- Nutrients
- Sauternes yeast starter
- Water to 22.5 quarts (20 liters)
- 1 oz. (30 g.) pectic enzyme

METHOD

Peel the bananas (discarding the skins) and cut into slices. Boil the slices in 10 quarts (9 liters) of water for half an hour, and then strain the hot liquor over the washed pitted peaches. Add the nutrients, acids, glycerol, and honey and stir until dissolved. When cool, add the rose petals, pectic enzyme, and yeast starter. Ferment on the pulp for 2-3 days, then strain off the latter and press lightly. Add the grape concentrate, mix in thoroughly, and make up the volume to 22.5 quarts (20 liters) with water. Proceed as instructed in the basic method.

Graves (1)

INGREDIENTS

- 4 lb. (1.8 kg.) sugar beet
- 20 fl. oz. (570 ml.) white grape concentrate
- 10 fl. oz. (280 ml.) elderflowers
- ½ oz. (10 g.) tartaric acid
- 1 lb. (450 g.) honey
- Nutrients
- Bordeaux yeast starter
- Water to 5 quarts (4.5 liters)

METHOD

Wash the sugar beet, cut into chunks, and boil in 7.5 pints (4 liters) of water for half an hour. Strain off the pulp and add the honey, nutrients, and acids to the hot liquor. When cool, add the elderflowers, grape concentrate, and yeast starter. Ferment on the pulp for 2 days, then strain off the pulp and make up to 5 quarts (4.5 liters) with water. Continue as directed in the basic method.

Graves (2)

INGREDIENTS

- 4 lb. (1.8 kg.) greengages
- 2 lb. (900 g.) sultanas (seedless white grapes)
- 10 fl. oz. (280 ml.) yellow rose petals
- 1 lb. (450 g.) sugar
- Nutrients
- Bordeaux yeast starter
- Water to 5 quarts (4.5 liters)
- ½ oz. (15 g.) pectic enzyme

METHOD

Pit the greengages, chop the sultanas (seedless white grapes), and scald with 7.5 pints (4 liters) of boiling water. Add the sugar and nutrients while still hot and stir until dissolved. When cool, add the rose petals, pectic enzyme, and yeast starter. Ferment on the pulp for 3 days, then strain off the latter and press lightly. Make up the volume to 5 quarts (4.5 liters) with the water and continue as instructed in the basic method.

Graves (3)

INGREDIENTS

- 2 lb. (900 g.) sultanas (seedless white grapes)
- 2.5 pints (1.1 liters) dandelion petals
- ¼ oz. (10 g.) tartaric acid
- ¼ oz. (10 g.) malic acid
- 2 lb. (900 g.) honey
- Nutrient
- Bordeaux yeast starter
- Water to 5 quarts (4.5 liters)

METHOD

Pick the dandelions on a dry sunny day and cut off the petals, rejecting the green calices. Add 2 lb. (900 g) chopped sultanas (seedless white grapes) to every 2.5 pints (1.1 liters) of petals and add 8.75 pints (4.25 liters) of boiling water. Add the nutrients, acids, and honey and stir until dissolved. When cool, add the yeast starter. Ferment on the pulp for 2 days then strain off the latter and press lightly. Make up the volume to 5 quarts (4.5 liters) with water and proceed as directed in the basic method.

Graves (4)

INGREDIENTS

- 4 lb. (1.8 kg.) peaches
- 2.5 pints (1.1 liters) gorse flowers
- 20 fl. oz. (570 ml.) white grape concentrate
- ⅓ oz. (10 g.) tartaric acid
- ½ oz. (15 g.) pectic enzyme
- 1 lb. (450 g.) honey
- Nutrients
- Bordeaux yeast starter
- Water to 5 quarts (4.5 liters)

METHOD

Pit the peaches, add the gorse flowers, and add 7.5 pints (4 liters) of boiling water. Add the honey, acid, and nutrients until dissolved. When cool, add the pectic enzyme and yeast starter. Ferment on the pulp for 3 days, then strain off the latter and press lightly. Add the grape concentrate and make the volume up to 5 quarts (4.5 liters) with water. Proceed as directed in the basic method.

Graves (5)

22.5 quarts (20 liters)

INGREDIENTS

- 20 lb. (9 kg.) peaches
- 4 lb. (1.8 kg.) bananas
- 2 lb. (900 g.) raisins
- 2.5 pints (1.1 liters) white grape concentrate
- 2.5 pints (1.1 liters) elderflowers
- ½ oz. (15 g.) tartaric acid
- ½ oz. (15 g.) malic acid
- 4 lb. (1.8 kg.) sugar
- 1 oz. (30 g.) pectic enzyme
- Nutrients
- Bordeaux yeast starter
- Water to 22.5 quarts (20 liters)

METHOD

Peel the bananas (discarding the skins) and cut into slices. Boil the slices in 5 quarts (4.5 liters) of water for half an hour, and then strain the hot liquor over the pitted peaches and raisins. Add 7.5 quarts (6 liters) of boiling water and dissolve the acids, nutrients, and sugar in the hot liquor. When cool, add the elderflowers, pectic enzyme, and yeast starter. Ferment on the pulp for 3 days, then strain off the latter and press lightly. Add the grape concentrate and make the volume up to 22.5 quarts (20 liters) with water. Continue as instructed in the basic method.

Bordeaux Blanc

INGREDIENTS

- 4 lb. (1.8 kg.) parsnips
- One 20-fl.-oz. (570-ml.) can pineapple juice
- 10 fl. oz. (280 ml.) white grape concentrate
- 1½ lb. (675 g.) honey
- ¼ teaspoon (5 g.) grape tannin
- ¼ oz. (10 g.) pectic enzyme
- ¼ oz. (10 g.) tartaric acid
- Yeast nutrients
- Bordeaux yeast starter
- Water to 5 quarts (4.5 liters)

METHOD

Chop and boil parsnips in 6.25 pints (3 liters) of water for 20 minutes, and strain liquor over pineapple juice, grape concentrate, honey, tannin, and acid. When cool, add the pectic enzyme, yeast nutrient, and active yeast starter. Strain off any pulp fragments after 3 days and continue as in basic method.

Chapter 7

CHIANTI (NEW AND OLD)

Chianti is the best-known Italian wine, and, as a result, there is a tendency to label all Italian dry wines as Chianti. Strictly speaking, however, Chianti comes from the Italian province of Tuscany, the area around the cities of Florence, Pisa, Arezzo, and Siena.

Life is still somewhat harsh for the Italian peasant, and in his efforts to extract a living from the soil, he tends to crowd crops together. Thus, vines trained on pergolas are found growing in between other crops, and in fact they are often trained up trees and houses. Wherever there is a space, put in a vine is the policy of most growers, but grapes grown this way do not tend to produce high-quality wines. Visitors to Italy will find that much of the local Chianti has a rough astringent taste, with a grip on the tongue as though one were chewing oak bark. This is old-style Chianti, and some people like it, for it can become an acquired taste, so we have included some recipes for it in this section.

The leading Tuscan growers have, however, made strenuous efforts in recent years to raise the standard of Chianti to a much higher level. These new-style Chiantis are smooth full-bodied dry wines and are more refined than the older-style types, although in many cases they are still a little more astringent than comparable French red wines. They are often bottled in ordinary wine bottles rather than in the wicker flagons that one normally associates with Chianti.

Their labels bear the emblems of a black rooster on a gold background. To produce wine of this type is not too difficult, and once the correct blend of ingredients is chosen, there are no special techniques involved. The normal winemaking procedure is all that is necessary.

White Chianti is plentiful, but because it is not rated very highly, we have not made provision for recipes of this type. Overall, these wines are indistinguishable from any of the carafe wines one comes across anywhere in Europe.

One additional type of Chianti deserves attention. These wines are called Frizzantes, a name that indicates they are sparkling. They are, nevertheless, not frothy like champagne, for that superb wine Asti Spumante fulfills that role. They are made by what is called the governo process. In this process, small amounts of fresh grape juice are added to the wine just when the fermentation is all but finished. The wine is bottled shortly after this,

so that a very small secondary fermentation occurs inside the bottle. Of course, because the wine is not dealt with in the manner of champagne, there is a small yeast deposit in each bottle, but no one seems to mind if the last couple of glasses are a little cloudy. Indeed, yeast is said to be excellent for the complexion and these glasses are often given to the ladies on this pretext.

A hydrometer is essential for the production of Frizzante wines and we would not recommend anyone try to make them without its aid, in case exploding bottles are the result. There are, in fact, three ways one can approach the problem. First, one can follow the Italian method and add syrup or grape concentrate when the fermentation is finished and one has ascertained with the hydrometer that the specific gravity has fallen well below the 1.000 mark.

The amount to add would be 5 fluid ounces (150 milliliters) of grape concentrate, or syrup that has a specific gravity of 48, to every 5 quarts (4.5 liters) of wine.

This addition should be made about 3-4 weeks after the first racking, and the wine is then immediately racked once more and bottled with ordinary straight wine corks, but the corks should not be wired down. The bottles should be stored upright in case a slight error of judgment has occurred and the corks blow out.

The second method is to rack the wine when it has fallen just below the 1.000 mark and to sulfate the wine with 50 ppm sulfur dioxide (one Campden tablet per 5 quarts, 4.5 liters), leave the wine for a few days to clear somewhat, and then to bottle. There is a slightly greater risk of corks blowing out here and they must be watched and replaced if they do.

Do not tie the corks, but just replace them. Eventually the amount of carbon dioxide will be insufficient to force out the corks while still being enough to provide a sparkle.

The safest way to ensure the right amount of sugar is to test the wine after racking with a Clinitest or other sugar-level test kit (available from chemists). The Clinitest is used by diabetics, and, with its help, one can tell in a few seconds what percentage of sugar is left in the wine. The wine should be bottled when the test indicates that between ¼ percent and ½ percent is left in the wine.

Basic Method

In the recipes that follow, quantities are given for 22.5-quart (20-liter) ferments, because for all dry red wines it is best to make this quantity at least and to mature the wine in a cask. The quantities should be scaled down accordingly if 5 quarts (4.5 liters.) are required as would normally be the case for Frizzante wines.

1. Prepare the ingredients as indicated in each recipe.

2. When the fermentation has ceased, the wine should be racked off the lees into a fresh container, preferably a cask, and then

be racked every 4 months. Evaporation losses can be replaced with water or a mixture of water and wine. The wine should be matured in this way for at least 6 months, for an old-style Chianti, or a year, for a new-style Chianti, before bottling.

3. If a Frizzante wine is required, proceed in one of the following ways (note that Frizzante wine can be made from any of the recipes listed in this chapter):
   a) Test the fermentation with a hydrometer, and when the reading is below 1.000 (say 0.995), add one Campden tablet per 5 quarts (4.5 liters), rack, and bottle 4-7 days later, leaving 1½ inches (25 millimeters) below the cork. Store in a cool place and check the corks daily for a week or so and then occasionally, replacing them if they blow out. The wine should be kept a year before drinking.
   b) Test the fermenting wine in its final stages with a Clinitest or other sugar-level test kit, and when test indicates the wine contains ¼-½ a percent sugar, rack and bottle as before.
   c) Test the fermenting wine with a hydrometer, racking when it falls below the 1.000 mark. Rack again 3 weeks later and add syrup or grape concentrate of specific gravity 48 (approximately ¼ pound (110 grams) of sugar boiled up with 20 fluid ounces (570 milliliters) of water) at the rate of 5 fluid ounces (150 milliliters) of this syrup to every 5 quarts (4.5 liters) of wine. Bottle as before.

Recipe 1 (Old-style)
INGREDIENTS

- 9 lb. (4 kg.) elderberries
- 9 lb. (4 kg.) raisins
- 2.5 pints (1.1 liters) red grape concentrate
- 4 lb. (1.8 kg.) honey
- Yeast nutrients
- Chianti yeast starter
- Water to 22.5 quarts (20 liters)

METHOD
Crush the elderberries and raisins and scald with 17.5 quarts (15 liters) of boiling water. Stir in the honey and yeast nutrients. When cool, add the yeast starter and ferment on the pulp for 3 days. Strain off the pulp and press lightly. Add the grape concentrate and make up the volume to 22.5 quarts (20 liters) with cold water. Proceed as directed in the basic method.

Recipe 2 (Old-style)
INGREDIENTS

- 14 lb. (6.25 kg.) damsons
- 3 lb. (1.3 kg.) bananas
- 2.5 pints (1.1 liters) red grape concentrate
- 6 lb. (2.7 kg.) sugar
- 1 oz. (30 g.) pectic enzyme
- Yeast nutrients
- Chianti yeast starter
- Water to 22.5 quarts (20 liters)

METHOD
Peel the bananas (discarding the skins) and cut into slices. Boil the slices in 5 quarts (4.5 liters) of water for half an hour, and then strain the hot liquor over the pitted damsons. Add 12.5 quarts (10 liters) of boiling water and stir in the sugar and yeast nutrients. When cool, add the pectic enzyme and yeast starter. Ferment on the pulp for 4-5 days, then strain off the pulp and press lightly. Add the grape concentrate and make up the volume to 22.5 quarts (20 liters) with cold water. Continue as instructed in the basic method.

Recipe 3 (New-style)
INGREDIENTS
- 18 lb. (8 kg.) cherries
- 4 lb. (1.8 kg.) raisins
- 3 lb. (1.3 kg.) bananas
- 2.5 pints (1.1 liters) red grape concentrate
- 4 lb. (1.8 kg.) sugar or honey
- Yeast nutrients
- Chianti yeast starter
- Water to 22.5 quarts (20 liters)

METHOD
Peel the bananas (discarding the skins) and cut into slices. Boil the slices in about 5 quarts (4.5 liters) of water for half an hour, and then strain the hot liquor over the washed crushed cherries and raisins (cherry pits should not be broken). Add an additional 10 quarts (9 liters) of boiling water, together with the sugar or honey and yeast nutrients, and stir until dissolved. When cool, add the yeast starter. Ferment on the pulp for 4-5 days, then strain off the pulp and press lightly. Add the grape concentrate and make up the volume to 22.5 quarts (20 liters) with cold water. Continue as instructed in the basic method.

Recipe 4 (New-style)
INGREDIENTS
- 2 lb. (900 g.) dried elderberries
- 2 lb. (900 g.) dried bilberries
- 2 lb. (900 g.) raisins
- 2.5 pints (1.1 liters) red grape concentrate
- 5 lb. (2.25 kg.) honey
- Yeast nutrients
- Chianti yeast starter
- Water to 22.5 quarts (20 liters)

METHOD
Wash the elderberries, bilberries, and raisins and scald with 17.5 quarts (15 liters) of boiling water. Add the honey and yeast nutrients and stir until the honey has dissolved. When cool, add the yeast starter. Ferment on the pulp for 2 days, then strain off and pulp and press lightly. Add the grape concentrate and make up the volume to 22.5 quarts (20 liters) with cold water. Proceed as directed in the basic method.

Recipe 5 (Old-style)
INGREDIENTS
- 10 lb. (4.5 kg.) sloes
- 4 lb. (1.8 kg.) bananas
- 2 lb. (900 g.) raisins
- 2.5 pints (1.1 liters) red grape concentrate
- 5 lb. (2.25 kg.) sugar or honey
- Yeast nutrients
- Chianti yeast starter
- Water to 22.5 quarts (20 liters)

METHOD

Peel the bananas (discard the skins) and cut into slices. Boil the slices in about 5 quarts (4.5 liters) of water for half an hour, and then strain the hot liquor over the washed crushed sloes and raisins. Add another 10 quarts (9 liters) of boiling water, together with the sugar or honey and yeast nutrients, and stir until dissolved. When cool, add the yeast starter. Ferment on the pulp for 2-3 days, then strain off the pulp and press lightly. Add the grape concentrate and make up the volume to 22.5 quarts (20 liters) with cold water. Continue as directed in the basic method.

Recipe 6 (New-style)
INGREDIENTS

- 18 lb. (8 kg.) elderberries
- 4 lb. (1.8 kg.) bananas
- 5 pints (2.2 liters) red grape concentrate
- 3 lb. (1.3 kg.) honey or sugar
- Yeast nutrients
- Chianti yeast starter
- Water to 22.5 quarts (20 liters)

METHOD

Crush the elderberries and strain off the juice, keeping the pulp. Peel the bananas (discard the skins) and cut into slices. Boil the slices in 5 quarts (4.5 liters) of water for half an hour, and then strain the hot liquor over the elderberry pulp. Stir the latter for 5 minutes, then strain. Add another 5 quarts (4.5 liters) of boiling water to the elderberry pulp, stir for 5 minutes, and again strain. Reject the elderberry pulp. Add another 5 quarts (4.5 liters) of water to the banana and elderberry extract, together with the honey or sugar and yeast nutrients, and stir until dissolved. When cool, add the grape concentrate, sufficient water to bring the volume up to 22.5 quarts (20 liters), and the yeast starter. Ferment in the normal manner and finally proceed as directed in the basic method.

Chapter 8

MADEIRA-TYPE WINES

Madeira is a romantic wine, for the Portuguese island from which it takes its name is itself a largely unspoiled paradise with an ideal climate, a place of beautiful mountain ranges and lush vegetation. Many of the old winemaking methods are still practiced, and it is a common sight to see the freshly fermented wine being carried down the hillside in goatskins on the backs of carriers.

Madeira is really a group of four wines, and together they can cater with a complete meal from aperitif to liqueur. The amber wine Sercial is the driest of the four and has a nutty flavor that makes it an ideal aperitif. Next follows Verdelho, a golden-colored wine that is a little sweeter than Sercial, but has an aromatic bouquet that renders it suitable either as an aperitif or as a table wine. Bual, on the other hand, is a full-bodied medium-sweet tawny wine that is suitable for dessert or for general drinking. The last of the four, Malmsey, is perhaps the best known of the four types and was much loved by the English court circles in earlier days. It is a very lush deep tawny wine that can easily serve as a liqueur in discerning company.

Producing Madeira

In order to produce wines of the Madeira type, one needs the right ingredients, the right technique, and a certain amount of luck. The technique that is used to produce these wonderful wines of Madeira will normally ruin the wines of other lands, and similarly, any lack of balance in the amateur winemaker's must may produce a failure to some extent. However, it must be admitted that when things go right, the resultant Madeira-type wine is well worth the risk.

The range of ingredients from which Madeira-type wines can be made is a little limited and is primarily confined to the following: bananas, raisins, grape concentrate, sultanas (seedless white grapes), sugar beet, yellow plums, greengages, peaches, and parsnips. If the reader is contemplating some other ingredient,

it might well be suitable if it is not a deep red color (except perhaps blackberries, which lose their color fairly quickly) and if it does not have too much flavor of its own.

Next, an essential for success is a good Madeira yeast and a fermentation that is nurtured most carefully, with sugar additions (in syrup form) in very small doses. An ideal fermenting temperature is around 70°F (20°C), but after a few days a temperature of 65°F (17°C) is even better, for this will ensure a long slow fermentation (in Madeira this lasts as long as 10 weeks before racking). Under these conditions, 18 percent alcohol by volume (31 proof) can be obtained without too much difficulty.

Once the wine has fermented out, and has been racked into fresh containers, there follows the estufagem process, which really means that the wine is heated for a long period.

The temperatures used in Madeira are as follows:
- Best wines, 90°-100°F (32°-38°C) for up to a year
- Superior wines, 100°-110°F (38°-43°C) for 6 months
- Ordinary grades, 120°F (49°C) for 4½ months
- Cheapest wines 130°-140°F (54°-60°C) for 3 months

For the amateur winemaker, his estufa, or baking chamber, is anywhere where one of these temperatures can be maintained for the required time. Ideally, the temperature should not vary at all from day to day, but with the robust ingredients in our wines, this is less important than when dealing with the grape alone. Some people have a stove or radiator that is always hot in the winter and above which the wine can be stored. An insulated box heated with an electric light bulb, like the ones used by amateur tobacco growers for curing, will also suffice. Given a warm summer, a shed or garage will do if the wine is wrapped up on cooler nights with a bit of blanket. A thermostatically controlled fermentation cupboard in which a constant temperature can be maintained indefinitely is, of course, ideal for the purpose.

The wine is simply left in these temperatures in demijohn jars (allowing for a little expansion and for a temporary renewal of fermentation until the yeast is killed by the heat). Evaporation losses are very small, but a miniature bottle of brandy per 5 quarts (4.5 liters) can be used to top off the small amount of lost alcohol.

When the wine has finished baking, it must be racked into fresh containers. At this stage it will, and should, taste awful. Many off flavors will have occurred, and most of these will become sublimated into finer flavors given time. Only one of these off flavors requires any treatment and that is the burnt sugar taste caused by excess caramelization of some residual sugar. This is easily cured by adding charcoal to the wine for a few days (about ½-1 oz. (15-30 g.) per 5 quarts, 4.5 liters), after which, the wine is again racked and left to mature.

This wine does require a fair amount of maturing and should not be made with the idea of early drinking. Cask maturing is of course better once one has acquired the technique and can risk larger quantities.

Basic Method

1. Proceed as directed in each recipe for the preparation of the must.

2. Check the specific gravity of the must regularly and add 5 fluid ounces (150 milliliters) of sugar syrup per 5 quarts (4.5 liters) whenever the specific gravity drops to 5 or less. This syrup is made by boiling up 2 pounds (900 grams) of sugar with 20 fluid ounces (570 milliliters) of water. For Sercial or Verdelho wines, do not add more sugar syrup when the fermentation slows down to the extent that a specific gravity drop of only 12 degrees per day is occurring. This will ensure a dry wine. For Bual and Malmsey wines, the sugar syrup additions should be continued until fermentation ceases and a sweet wine is obtained.

3. When the fermentation has ceased, allow the wine to settle for a few days and then rack it into demijohn jars.

4. Place the jars in a warm place, at one of the temperatures described previously and for the required time. There may be a little initial frothing for a few hours, after which, the jar can be topped up and left until the estufagem process has been completed.

5. Then, rack the wine into fresh jars or into casks and add ¼-1 ounce (10-30 grams) charcoal per 5 quarts (4.5 liters) for 3 days.

6. Rack the wine again and mature it until it is ready for drinking, which in some cases may be as long as 2 years.

Recipe 1 (Sercial or Verdelho)
INGREDIENTS

- 3 lb. (1.3 kg.) plums or greengages
- 1½ lb. (675 g.) bananas
- 20 fl. oz. (570 ml.) white grape concentrate
- ½ oz. (15 g.) tartaric acid
- ½ oz. (15 g.) pectic enzyme
- Yeast nutrients
- Madeira yeast starter
- Sugar as required
- Water to 5 quarts (4.5 liters)

METHOD

Peel the bananas and cut into slices (discard the skins). Boil the slices in 6.25 pints (3 liters) or water for half an hour, and then strain the hot liquor over the pitted plums or greengages. Add the tartaric acid and nutrients. When cool, add the pectic enzyme and yeast starter. Ferment on the pulp for 3-4 days, then strain off and press the pulp. Add the grape concentrate and sufficient sugar syrup to bring the volume up to about 8.75 quarts (4 liters). Follow the procedure as outlined in the basic method.

Recipe 2 (Sercial or Verdelho)
INGREDIENTS

- 3.75 pints (2 liters) dandelion petals
- 2 lb. (900 g.) bananas
- 20 fl. oz. (570 ml.) white grape concentrate
- 1 lb. (450 g.) honey
- ½ oz. (15 g.) tartaric acid
- Yeast nutrients
- Madeira yeast starter
- Sugar as required
- Water to 5 quarts (4.5 liters)

METHOD
Peel the bananas and cut into slices (discard the skins). Boil the slices in 6.25 pints (3 liters) of water for half an hour, and then strain the hot liquor over the dandelion petals and honey. Add the tartaric acid and nutrients. When cool, mix in 10 fl. oz. (280 ml.) of grape concentrate and add the yeast starter. Ferment on the flowers for 2 days, then strain off the pulp and press lightly. Add the rest of the grape concentrate and sufficient sugar syrup to bring the volume up to about 8.75 pints (4 liters). Continue as detailed in the basic method.

Recipe 3 (Sercial or Verdelho)
INGREDIENTS

- 4 lb. (1.8 kg.) peaches
- 1 lb. (450 g.) bananas
- 1½ lb. (675 g.) raisins
- ¾ oz. (20 g.) tartaric acid
- ½ oz. (15 g.) pectic enzyme
- Yeast nutrients
- Madeira yeast starter
- Sugar as required
- Water to 5 quarts (4.5 liters)

METHOD
Peel the bananas and cut into slices (discard the skins). Boil the slices in 6.25 pints (3 liters) of water for half an hour, and then strain the hot liquor over the washed raisins and pitted peaches. Add the tartaric acid and nutrients. When cool, add the pectic enzyme and yeast starter. Ferment on the pulp for 3 days, then strain off and press the pulp. Bring the volume up to about 8.75 pints (4 liters) with sugar syrup and water and then continue as instructed in the basic method.

Recipe 4 (Sercial or Verdelho)
INGREDIENTS

- 4 lb. (1.8 kg.) ripe gooseberries
- 2 lb. (900 g.) bananas
- 20 fl. oz. (570 ml.) white grape concentrate
- ¼ oz. (10 g.) tartaric acid
- ½ oz. (15 g.) pectic enzyme
- Yeast nutrients
- Madeira yeast starter
- Sugar as required
- Water to 5 quarts (4.5 liters)

METHOD
Peel the bananas and cut into slices (discard the skins). Boil the slices in 6.25 quarts (3 liters) of water for half an hour, and then strain the hot liquor over the crushed gooseberries. Add the tartaric acid and nutrients. When cool, add 10 fl. oz. (280 ml.) of grape concentrate, the pectic enzyme, and the yeast starter. Ferment on the pulp for 3 days, then strain off and press the pulp. Add the other 10 fl. oz. (280 ml.) of grape concentrate and sufficient sugar syrup to bring the volume up to about 8.75 quarts (4 liters). Proceed as directed in the basic method.

Recipe 5 (Sercial or Verdelho)

22.5 quarts (20 liters), cask maturing

INGREDIENTS

- 10 lb. (4.5 kg.) peaches
- 10 lb. (4.5 kg.) ripe gooseberries
- 9 lb. (4.25 kg.) bananas
- 2 lb. (900 g.) raisins
- 3.75 pints (3.3 liters) white grape concentrate
- 1 oz. (30 g.) tartaric acid
- 1 oz. (30 g.) pectic enzyme
- Yeast nutrients
- Madeira yeast starter
- Sugar as required
- Water to 22.5 quarts (20 liters)

METHOD

Peel the bananas and cut into slices (discard the skins). Boil the slices in 12.5 quarts (10 liters) of water for half an hour, and then strain the hot liquor over the pitted peaches, crushed gooseberries, and washed raisins. Add the tartaric acid and nutrients. When cool, mix in 20 fl. oz. (570 ml.) of grape concentrate and add the pectic enzyme and yeast starter. Ferment on the pulp for 3 days, then strain off and press the pulp. Add the rest of the grape concentrate and a sufficient amount of sugar syrup to bring the volume up to about 18.75 quarts (18 liters). Proceed as instructed in the basic method. Cask maturing after heat treatment (and charcoal treatment, if necessary) is recommended.

Recipe 6 (Sercial or Verdelho)

22.5 quarts (20 liters), cask maturing

INGREDIENTS

- 18 lb. (8 kg.) greengages or yellow plums
- 9 lb. (4.5 kg.) bananas
- 3 packets (165 g.) dried dandelion petals
- 2 lb. (900 g.) raisins
- 3.75 pints (3.3 liters) white grape concentrate
- 1½ oz. (45 g.) tartaric acid
- 1 oz. (30 g.) pectic enzyme
- Yeast nutrients
- Madeira yeast starter
- Sugar as required
- Water to 22.5 quarts (20 liters)

METHOD

Peel the bananas and cut into slices (discard the skins). Boil the slices in 12.5 quarts (10 liters) of water for half an hour, and then strain the hot liquor over the dandelion petals, washed raisins, and pitted greengages. Add the tartaric acid and nutrients. When cool, add the pectic enzyme and yeast starter. Ferment on the pulp for 3 days, then strain off and press the pulp. Add the grape concentrate and sufficient sugar syrup to bring the volume up to 18.75 quarts (18 liters). Continue as directed in the basic method. Cask maturing after heat treatment (and charcoal treatment, if necessary) is recommended.

Recipe 7 (Bual or Malmsey)
INGREDIENTS

- 6 lb. (2.7 kg.) blackberries
- 2 lb. (900 g.) bananas
- 20 fl. oz. (570 ml.) white grape concentrate
- ½ oz. (15 g.) pectic enzyme
- Yeast nutrients
- Madeira yeast starter
- Sugar as required
- Water to 5 quarts (4.5 liters)

METHOD

Peel the bananas and cut into slices (discard the skins). Boil the slices in 6.25 pints (3 liters) of water for half an hour, and then strain the hot liquor over the crushed blackberries. Add the nutrients. When cool, add the pectic enzyme and yeast starter. Ferment on the pulp for 2 days and then strain off and press the pulp lightly. Add the grape concentrate and a sufficient amount of sugar syrup to bring the volume up to about 8.75 pints (4 liters). Proceed as instructed in the basic method.

Recipe 8 (Bual or Malmsey)
INGREDIENTS

- 4 lb. (1.8 kg.) parsnips
- 2 lb. (900 g.) bananas
- 20 fl. oz. (570 ml.) white grape concentrate
- ½ oz. (15 g.) tartaric acid
- ½ oz. (15 g.) pectic enzyme
- Yeast nutrients
- Madeira yeast starter
- Sugar as required
- Water to 5 quarts (4.5 liters)

METHOD

Peel the bananas and cut into slices (discard the skins). Boil the slices in 6.25 pints (3 liters) of water for half an hour, together with the washed sliced parsnips. Strain off carefully and add the tartaric acid and nutrients. When cool, add the grape concentrate, pectic enzyme, and yeast starter, together with a sufficient amount of sugar syrup to bring the volume up to about 8.75 pints (4 liters). Proceed as directed in the basic method.

Recipe 9 (Bual or Malmsey)
INGREDIENTS

- 6 lb. (2.7 kg.) ripe gooseberries
- 2 lb. (900 g.) bananas
- 2 lb. (900 g.) raisins
- ¼ oz. (10 g.) tartaric acid
- ¼ oz. (10 g.) pectic enzyme
- Yeast nutrients
- Madeira yeast starter
- Sugar as required
- Water to 5 quarts (4.5 liters)

METHOD

Peel the bananas and cut into slices (discard the skins). Boil the slices in 6.75 pints (3 liters) of water for half an hour, and then strain the hot liquor over the washed raisins and crushed gooseberries. Add the nutrients and tartaric acid. When cool, add the pectic enzyme and yeast starter. Ferment on the pulp for 3 days, then strain off the pulp and press lightly. Add 10 fl. oz. (280 ml.) of water and a sufficient amount of sugar syrup to bring the volume up to about 8.75 pints (4 liters). Continue as directed in the basic method.

Recipe 10 (Bual or Malmsey)

INGREDIENTS

- 2 lb. (900 g.) bananas
- 1 lb. (450 g.) dried apricots
- 20 fl. oz. (570 ml.) white grape concentrate
- ½ oz. (15 g.) pectic enzyme
- Yeast nutrients
- Madeira yeast starter
- Sugar as required
- Water to 5 quarts (4.5 liters)

METHOD

Peel the bananas and cut into slices (discard the skins). Boil the slices and dried apricots in 6.75 pints (3 liters) of water for half an hour, then strain off and press lightly. Add the nutrients and, when cool, add the pectic enzyme and yeast starter. After 2 days, add the grape concentrate and a sufficient amount of sugar syrup to bring the volume up to about 8.75 pints (4 liters). Proceed as instructed in the basic method.

Recipe 11 (Malmsey or Bual)

22.5 quarts (20 liters), cask maturing

INGREDIENTS

- 18 lb. (8 kg.) peaches
- 9 lb. (4 kg.) ripe gooseberries
- 9 lb. (4 kg.) bananas
- 4 lb. (1.8 kg.) raisins
- 2.5 pints (1.1 liters) white grape concentrate
- 4 lb. (1.8 kg.) honey
- ½ oz. (15 g.) tartaric acid
- 1 oz. (30 g.) pectic enzyme
- Nutrients
- Madeira yeast starter
- Sugar as required
- Water to 22.5 quarts (20 liters)

METHOD

Peel the bananas and cut into slices (discard the skins). Boil the slices in about 13.75 quarts (13 liters) of water for half an hour, and then strain the hot liquor over the crushed gooseberries, pitted peaches, washed raisins, and honey. Add the tartaric acid and nutrients. When cool, add the pectic enzyme and yeast starter. Ferment on the pulp for 3 days and then strain off and press the pulp lightly. Add the grape concentrate and a sufficient amount of sugar syrup to bring the volume up to about 18.75 quarts (18 liters). Proceed as directed in the basic procedure. Cask maturing after heat treatment is recommended.

Chapter 9

ROSÉ WINES

One often is asked about *vin rosé*, and it is a type of wine that seems to stir people's imagination. Its beautiful color, ranging from delicate pink to almost red, goes well with both sunlight and candlelight, so that it is equally acceptable in summer or winter. Also, it can be drunk at almost any time of day with satisfaction, and in quantity without undue intoxication.

We have a friend, blind from birth, who recently started making wine. In order to give him an idea of the types of wines he might expect from different ingredients, a tasting was arranged, in the course of which he tasted both white and red wines and quickly discerned their difference in character by taste alone, because red and white meant nothing to him. On being given a rosé wine, he remarked that it did not differ very much from the white wines and was certainly quite unlike the reds.

This profound observation was once often rediscovered by wine judges upon encountering a rosé wine among a class of red wines. The unfortunate rosé was so different from the rest of the class that it rarely stood a chance of gaining an award. This anomaly has had to be resolved, and rosé wines are now usually assigned a separate class of their own.

Most winemaking areas of Europe produce rosé wines, and apart from minor local practices, the method of production is fundamentally the same. It is because the coloring matter in a grape is generally localized in the skin and does not dissolve easily in grape juice, although it does so quite readily in dilute solutions of alcohol, such as fermenting wine musts. Thus, if either red or white grapes are pressed, the juice expressed is white and a white wine will result.

If, however, black grapes are fermented on the pulp, the must rapidly darkens in color, and after about 4 or 5 days of such a fermentation, enough color has been extracted to make the finished wine deep red. At the same time, a considerable amount of tannin is extracted, which gives a red wine its characteristic bite. Rosé wines are made in the same way, but the period of pulp fermentation is restricted to a period varying between 6 hours and 48 hours according to the degree of color and astringency required.

There are other ways of producing rosé wines, but nearly always these produce wines of an inferior quality. For instance,

in some parts of Europe, *vin rosé* is made simply by blending a white wine with a small portion of red wine. Such a blend rarely marries well and the lack of homogeneity is recognized upon tasting the wine. It is even possible to make *vin rosé* from a certain type of grape called a Teinturier, which has a reddish-purple pulp and yields a reddish juice. This type of *vin rosé* is quite common in Algeria, but very little of it is exported.

Best Rosés

Some of the best rosé wines, mostly quite light in color, are produced in the Loire valley of France, those of Anjou, Saumur, and Touraine being the best-known. They are good honest wines bottled about 6 months after fermentation in order to preserve their freshness and fragrance and generally drunk within the year, although they tend to improve for a further 2 years in the bottle. They are mostly made from Cabernet or Groslot grapes, although there is a wine, Pinot Rosé de Sancerre (made from Pinot Noir grapes), which is very much sought after and can be quite difficult to obtain.

Wines of a similar nature are made in the Basses Pyrenees (rosé de Béarn) and in Portugal, where the increasingly popular Mateus Rosé is produced. This latter wine is gaining popularity through its sheer merit, rather than through any form of advertising, and it has the additional attraction of being slightly sparkling, not effervescent like champagne, but with bubbles hugging the sides of the glass, and having a slightly prickly taste.

Deep-colored rosé wines are produced in the Burgundy district, further south in the Rhône valley, and generally in the Mediterranean area (Algeria, Corsica, Yugoslavia, Spain, and Portugal). In most cases, the period of pulp fermentation extends to 48 hours, varying with local practice and the type of grape. Many of these are either poor in quality or made in such small quantities that they rarely reach the rest of the world. One exception, however, is Tavel Rosé, said by some to be the finest rosé wine in the world. It is made from a variety of *cépages*, notably the Grenache and Cinsault vines that, along with others, are used in making the great red wine of the Rhône valley, Châteauneuf-du-Pape.

A very deep rosé called Clairet is made in the Bordeaux region. It is typical of the type of Bordeaux shipped to Britain during the Middle Ages before the much superior claret was produced. This type of wine (labeled Clairet, Bordeaux Rosé, or simply Vin Rosé) is of interest in that it provides a useful standard of comparison for the amateur, even though it is of no great interest commercially. If the winemaker can produce rosé wines of comparable quality, he can rest assured in his ability in this field of winemaking.

The Pink Problem

The problem facing amateur winemakers is not in producing a pink or light-red wine, for this is extremely simple. The difficulty is in achieving the fresh fruity flavor and bouquet associated with rosé wines. This fruity freshness is, however, not strongly reminiscent of the ingredients of the must, but rather a characteristic of a young wine. Having achieved these factors, of course, great care is necessary to avoid losing them again during racking and maturing.

Fruits that lend themselves well to this fruity aspect of rosé wine production are red currants, rhubarb, apricots, cherries, green gooseberries, peaches, rose hips, and white grape concentrate. Strawberries are also of use, provided cold extraction methods are used in preparing the must and great care given to the finished wine. The rosé color can be achieved or intensified best by the addition of a little red grape concentrate.

Most rosé wines are around 10-11 percent alcohol by volume and typically lose their character if made any stronger, so a starting gravity of only about 80 is required. The acidity of the pink rosés of the Loire type is between 3.5 and 4.0 ppt (in terms of sulfuric acid measurement), but the majority of the acid present is malic, and this type of wine cannot be made if this acidity is achieved with the harsher-tasting tartaric and citric acids alone. The acidity of the deeper-colored rosés is lower (between 3.0 and 3.5 ppt), but here the greater part of the acid is tartaric, the remainder being malic.

FERMENTATION CARE

Care in handling the fermentation is perhaps the most important factor, once a suitable blend of fruits is available. Cold water extraction or pressing is practically essential and this in turn involves the use of sulfite (Campden tablets). A fairly cool fermentation, 65°-70°F (18°-22°C), is a distinct advantage to avoid dissipation of fragrance. Because this may involve a slightly longer period of fermentation, it is necessary to make sure that the initial must is as clean as possible, i.e., does not contain pulp fragments that might disintegrate during the fermentation period.

RACKING CAUTION

Racking also should be done very carefully, with not too great a distance between the two jars, and without splashing. At each racking, the wine should be sulfated with a Campden tablet per 5 quarts (4.5 liters), or 50 ppm, at least—some commercial rosés being kept almost permanently under 75 ppm sulfur dioxide during the whole period of their maturing. Generally, the finished wines should be bottled for 2 or 2 months at least before being consumed. This allows the last vestiges of the sulfur dioxide to vanish and for the natural bouquet and flavor to reassert itself. The wine is best lightly chilled before being consumed.

ENZYME USE

Finally, a good case can be made out for the use of a pectin-destroying enzyme preparation such as Rohament P, Pectinol, or Pectolase in making these wines.

The period of maturation is so short, in order to preserve the fruity freshness, that there is no time to be lost in obtaining a brilliantly clear wine. Filtration would be disastrous to such a wine and even finings leave much to be desired in this case. It is infinitely preferable to add a small quantity of one of the above-mentioned preparations to the must at the same time as entering the yeast. A heaping teaspoon of the enzyme preparation per 5 quarts (4.5 liters) is quite sufficient at this stage, and one does not have to resort to the more massive additions sometimes required to clear a finished wine that is hazy.

Basic Method

1. Process the ingredients as indicated in each recipe.
2. Store the finished wine in a cool place and rack again when it is 3 months old and again 3 months later. At each racking, care should be taken to avoid splashing, the wine should be sulfated with one or two Campden tablets per 5 quarts (4.5 liters), and the jar should be topped up with wine or water. In the event of a heavy deposit forming that might seem to be pulp debris, rack earlier (even as close as two weeks after the first racking) and add one additional Campden tablet per 5 quarts (4.5 liters).
3. When the wine is 6 months old, it should be sulfated with 50 ppm sulfur dioxide (one Campden tablet per 5 quarts, 4.5 liters) and bottled.
4. The finished wine should be drinkable at this stage, but will normally improve in the bottle for a further 18 months.

Recipe 1
INGREDIENTS
- 4 lb. (1.8 kg.) red currants
- 20 fl. oz. (570 ml.) white grape concentrate
- 10 fl. oz. (280 ml.) red rose petals
- Nutrients
- Bordeaux yeast
- 1¼ lb. (550 g.) clover honey
- Water to 5 quarts (4.5 liters)

METHOD

Crush the red currants and add 7.5 pints (3.5 liters) of cold water in which the honey and nutrients have been dissolved. Add 100 ppm sulfite (two Campden tablets) and leave covered for 24 hours before introducing the yeast starter. Ferment on the pulp for 3 days and then strain it off and press lightly. Add the grape concentrate and make the volume up to 5 quarts (4.5 liters) with water. After another 4 days, add the rose petals and ferment on the flowers for 3 days before straining them off. The wine at this stage should possess a good rosé color. Rack for the first time when the specific gravity drops to just below 0. Add 50 ppm sulfite (one Campden tablet) and rack again as soon as fermentation restarts or a heavy deposit forms, whichever happens first. Proceed as directed in the basic method.

Recipe 2
INGREDIENTS

- 4 lb. (1.8 kg.) green gooseberries
- 10 fl. oz. (280 ml.) red grape concentrate
- 10 fl. oz. (280 ml.) elderflowers
- Nutrients
- Bordeaux yeast
- 1½ lb. (675 g.) sugar
- Water to 5 quarts (4.5 liters)

METHOD

Top and tail the gooseberries and add 7.5 pints (3.5 liters) of hot water together with the sugar and nutrients. Add 100 ppm sulfite (two Campden tablets) and leave covered for 24 hours. After this time, the gooseberries will have softened and should be crushed before introducing the yeast starter. Ferment on the pulp for 3 days, then strain it off and press lightly. Add the grape concentrate and make the volume up to 5 quarts (4.5 liters) with water. After another 4 days, add the elderflower and ferment on the flowers for 3 days before straining them off. Rack for the first time at a specific gravity of 0. Add 50 ppm sulfite (one Campden tablet) and proceed as directed in the basic method.

Recipe 3
INGREDIENTS

- 2 lb. (900 g.) peaches
- 1 lb. (450 g.) elderberries
- 10 fl. oz. (280 ml.) white grape concentrate
- 10 fl. oz. (280 ml.) red rose petals
- 1½ lb. (675 g.) sugar
- Nutrients
- Burgundy yeast
- Water to 5 quarts (4.5 liters)

METHOD

Pit the peaches and press out the juice. Crush the elderberries and add to the peach juice. Add 6.25 pints (3 liters) of water, in which the nutrients and sugar have been dissolved, and add 100 ppm sulfite (two Campden tablets). After 24 hours, introduce the yeast and ferment on the pulp until a light to medium rosé color develops (1-2 days), then strain off the pulp and press it lightly. After 4-5 days, add the grape concentrate and rose petals and ferment on the latter for 2-3 days, depending upon how deep a rosé color is desired. When the flowers are removed, make up the volume to 5 quarts (4.5 liters) with water and ferment to a specific gravity of just below 0. Rack at this stage, adding 50 ppm sulfite (one Campden tablet), and proceed as directed in the basic method.

Recipe 4
INGREDIENTS

- 4 oz. (110 g.) dried rose hip shells
- 1 lb. (450 g.) sultanas (seedless white grapes)
- 10 fl. oz. (280 ml.) red grape concentrate
- 10 fl. oz. (280 ml.) elderflowers
- ¼ oz. (10 g.) tartaric acid
- 1 lb. (450 g.) sugar
- Nutrients
- Bordeaux yeast
- ¼ oz. (10 g.) malic acid
- Water to 5 quarts (4.5 liters)

METHOD

Wash the rose hips and sultanas (seedless white grapes) and add 7.5 pints (3.5 liters) of water containing the nutrients, acids, and sugar. Add 100 ppm sulfite (two Campden tablets), and introduce the yeast 24 hours later. Ferment on the pulp for 3 days, then strain it off and press lightly. Add the grape concentrate and elderflowers and ferment on the latter for an additional 2-3 days. Make the volume up to 5 quarts (4.5 liters) with water and allow to ferment to dryness. Proceed as instructed in the basic method.

Recipe 5

INGREDIENTS

- 4 lb. (1.8 kg.) cherries
- 1 lb. (450 g.) sultanas (seedless white grapes)
- 10 fl. oz. (280 ml.) red rose petals
- Nutrients
- Burgundy yeast
- 1½ lb. (675 g.) clover honey
- Water to 5 quarts (4.5 liters)

METHOD

Crush the cherries, taking care not to break any pits. Add the washed sultanas (seedless white grapes) and 6.25 pints (3 liters) of water, containing the honey and nutrients. Add 100 ppm sulfite (two Campden tablets) and introduce the yeast starter after 24 hours. Ferment on the pulp for 3 days, then strain it off and press lightly. After another 4 days, add the rose petals and ferment on the flowers for 2-3 days. Make the volume up to 5 quarts (4.5 liters) with cold water and ferment to dryness. Continue as directed in the basic method.

Recipe 6

25 quarts (25 liters)

INGREDIENTS

- 3 lb. (1.3 kg.) dried apricots
- 1 lb. (450 g.) dried elderberries
- 2 lb. (900 g.) raspberries
- 2.5 pints (1.1 liters) white grape concentrate
- Rhône or Burgundy yeast
- 2.5 pints (1.1 liters) rose petals (mixed red and yellow)
- Nutrients
- 6 lb. (2.7 kg.) sugar
- Water to 25 quarts (25 liters)

METHOD

Wash the apricots and elderberries and mix with the crushed raspberries. Add 20 quarts (18 liters) of cold water, containing the sugar, nutrients, and 100 ppm sulfite (ten Campden tablets, two for every 5 quarts, 4.5 liters). After 24 hours, introduce the yeast and ferment on the pulp for 2-3 days before straining it off and pressing lightly. Add the grape concentrate, and about 4 days later add the rose petals. Ferment on the flowers for 2-3 days, then strain them off and make the volume up to 25 quarts (25 liters) with water. Ferment until the specific gravity drops to 0. Rack and add 50 ppm sulfite (one Campden tablet per 5 quarts (4.5 liters). Rack again as soon as fermentation restarts or a heavy deposit is formed, whichever is the sooner. Continue as directed in the basic method.

Chapter 10

CHAMPAGNE AND SPARKLING WINES

A great many amateur winemakers in this country make champagne-type wines with great success and safety. It is nevertheless necessary to issue a preliminary warning that this is not a beginner's wine. Great pressure exists inside champagne bottles, as great or greater than the pressure in a car tire, and accidents do occur occasionally in even commercial champagne making.

This can be illustrated by relating what befell a man who used to live in the Old Kent Road area of London close to the Elephant and Castle. He did everything on a grandiose scale. When wishing to put a nail in a door on which to hang coats, he would use a 6-inch (152-millimeter) nail so the coats could be hung on both sides of the door. He had a grapevine growing dustily outside his backdoor, and one day he announced to his neighbors that he was "going to 'ave a bash" at making champagne. He sent his children scurrying hither and thither for bottles, yeast, sugar, etc., and soon had a ferment going, which he filtered and bottled after a couple of days of fermentation. In his grandiose manner, he acquired some outsize corks, which he hammered into the bottles and then retired to bed well satisfied with his achievements. During the night, the corks shot the ceiling down, and when the winemaker came scampering down the stairs and stood amid the damp plaster debris, he said with emphasis, "You can't make wine from English grapes!"

Had he wired on the corks, the bottles would have burst, and it is this latter danger that made us hesitate a little before writing this champagne article.

Methods

There are several different methods of making champagne-type wines. The one outlined here has stood the test of time and has been used by amateur winemakers all over the country with a minimum risk of breakage. Some of the wines produced by this method are certainly up to the standard of the cheaper champagnes of commerce,

although none of them can of course hope to match the brilliance of quality that is experienced in vintage champagne.

Whether it is a fact with scientific reasons or merely a conditioning of our minds, champagne seems to have a different effect on the drinker from that of other wines. The bubbling effervescence of the wine seems to transmit its joy to the drinker, and people become light-hearted and even romantic. Under the influence of champagne, elderly people feel a temporary return of the vitality and *joie de vivre* of their youth.

SPARKLING WINES

Sparkling wines have been made for centuries all over the world, and many readers will be familiar with the Italian wine Asti Spumante, the Portuguese Mateus Rosé, sparkling Anjou from the Loire, and sparkling white Burgundy. In earlier days, ingenious methods were used to trap the bubbles of carbon dioxide, and special stout-walled casks were used, bunged down tight.

It is probable that sparkling wines were made more or less accidentally at first. In the past, wines were generally drunk soon after fermentation, within months, because otherwise, with their low alcoholic content and poor methods of storage, they would not keep. In some years, however, when the sun shone hot and long, the increased sugar content of the grapes resulted in a stronger wine that could be stored well into the following year. It was discovered that these wines often became sparkling and effervesced when opened.

Historical records suggest this was due to a second fermentation occurring in the bottle when the warmer weather returned. To some extent, this is true, but the high malic acid content of the grapes in the northern vineyards leads one to suspect that malolactic fermentation was also partly responsible. Many winemakers will have experienced this occasionally when opening a bottle of wine that was perfectly stable when bottled.

DOM PERIGNON

The great genius in champagne making was a Benedictine monk named Dom Perignon, who was as far ahead of his time scientifically in the wine world as was Leonardo da Vinci in his sphere. The methods he introduced, following his appointment as cellarman to the Abbey of Haut-Villiers in the Champagne district of France, were so good, that even today only minor improvements have been made.

The obvious scientific method he came across was the use of the bark of the cork oak to effectively seal bottles. This invention has of course affected the entire wine world, because corks have become the standard method of sealing bottles. Another invention of his, less obvious, but more significant from the point of view of champagne, was the development of a blending system that is the basis of the present-day cuvée method, which is mainly responsible for the gradual emergence of champagne as the outstanding sparkling wine, head and shoulders above every other type of sparkling wine.

We are talking here of the best champagnes, of course, for the poorer champagnes can sometimes be surpassed by the sparkling wines of other regions of France or other countries. There are so many factors involved in champagne making that the chances of error are greater than in the other wines. As a result, champagne is either superb or poor, but rarely mediocre. The poorer champagnes are the ones that we buy at a fairy low cost per bottle for parties in order to liven things up rapidly. The superb champagnes are well over twice the price, and are eagerly sought by connoisseurs, and drunk as they should be as a table wine right through the meal.

TANK FERMENTATION

There are three main methods of producing wines of the champagne type. The principal one of these, for producing large quantities of cheap champagne, is by tank fermentation. This is not of value to the amateur winemaker, because we do not have at our disposal the means with which to emulate it.

ADDING CARBON DIOXIDE

The second method is by artificially impregnating a stable still wine with carbon dioxide. This procedure produces moderately good results provided the basic wine is a good one. The wine, already matured and cleared, is drawn off into champagne bottles, dosed with spirit or brandy, and impregnated with carbon dioxide by means of a special machine. Facilities for amateurs to do this are comparatively limited, and in practice it is hardly worthwhile, although some successful methods have been published.

The carbon dioxide bottle on the market today, will produce a poor man's champagne in a minute. Fill the wine bottle about three-quarters full with a chilled white wine. Insert the gas bottle and charge with carbon dioxide until the pressure release valve blows. Unscrew your gas bottle, release the pressure in the bottle, and then remove cap and pour out a quart (liter) of instant champagne.

BOTTLE FERMENTATION

The only really practicable method for the amateur is the original well-proven one of bottle fermentation. This genuine French method, laborious though it may be, always gives the best champagne in the end.

First let us look at the way the French do it. Only the choicest grapes are used and great care is taken that no moldy or unripe grapes are included. These grapes are then directly pressed, without any prior treatment or pulp fermentation, and this juice, known as the *cuvée*, forms the basis of this superb wine beloved of connoisseurs.

The juice is lightly sulfated and then is impregnated with a champagne yeast culture and fermented in vats for up to 8 weeks at a fairly cool temperature.

After 8-10 weeks, the wine is racked and then blended with the products of other vintages. This blending is of vital importance in order to even out the variations caused by climate, soil, etc., to produce a finished wine of constant high quality.

A little later, the wine is carefully filtered to remove all cloudy matter and is then dosed with sugar syrup and a special champagne yeast. The amount of sugar added is of vital importance in order to obtain the correct pressure of carbon dioxide inside the bottle.

SUGAR AND GAS PRESSURE

It has been found that half an ounce (16 grams) of sugar in every quart (liter) of wine will give a gas pressure of 4 atmospheres (55 pounds per square inch, or 25 kilograms per 25.4 millimeters squared), and that has been found to be best in practice. In amateur winemaking terms, this represents 2½-3 ounces (70-85 grams) of sugar per 5 quarts (4.5 liters), or half an ounce (15 grams) per bottle. Some leading amateur winemakers tend to use a little less than this, but it would seem that this is a satisfactory as well as safe quantity to add.

The addition of further sugar is to be avoided, for the pressure can then easily rise to greater pressures than the bottles can withstand. Champagne bottles, when new, are said to be able to withstand 8 atmospheres (about 95 pounds per square inch) pressure, but once used, and having collected a series of outside scratches, they are greatly weakened, so it is necessary to err on the side of safety.

The wine, now dosed with sugar syrup and yeast, is drawn off into thick glass bottles, filled to within 2.5 inches (63.5 millimeters) of the rim, and stoppered with good-quality corks that are carefully wired down.

The bottles are then laid at a slight angle in special racks called *pupitres* (desks), and the temperature is maintained at 65°F (18°C) so the desired bottle fermentation gets under way. After a couple of weeks, the temperature is lowered to 50°F (10°C) to avoid a build up of excessive pressure in the bottles. The wine is now left for 1-3 years to mature, according to quality, during which time the wine is in contact with the yeast. The minimum period of 1 year of maturation is legally enforced in France.

DAILY TWIST

For the first 2 months, the bottles are given a slight twist every day and are gradually angled more and more so that eventually they are standing on their heads. This process, known as *rémuage*, is carried out in order to bring the yeast sediment down onto the cork, leaving the champagne clear above it.

At this point, the mass of yeast settled on the cork has to be removed, a process known as *dégorgement*. So this can be done without disturbing the sediment or losing the carbon dioxide gas, the bottles are first chilled and then the wiring is removed. The cork shoots out and the bottles are turned upright and lightly corked. When a series of bottles have been treated in this way, each bottle receives a dose of brandy or brandy and syrup, depending on the required sweetness of the finished champagne, after which, they are again corked down and wired, leaving an air space of about ¾ inch (20 millimeters) between the wine and the bottom of the cork.

Another method of *dégorgement* in use is to employ a freezing bath held at the temperature of -4°F (-20°C), by means of which the wine in the neck of the bottle is frozen and an ice plug of frozen wine and yeast sediment is ejected with the cork.

Adapting for Amateurs

It is not too difficult to adapt the commercial method to meet amateur winemakers' needs. It is, however, necessary to impress on readers that champagne making cannot be done casually. The work is a labor of love, and this can only be achieved when one becomes dedicated to champagne making as a hobby in its own right, and not just as a means to an end.

We would not ourselves attempt to make champagne without the aid of a hydrometer and some sugar testing kit, such as the Clinitest. In the following two methods described, the use of these aids is mentioned alongside the general instructions.

Method 1

1. Prepare the must in the usual way as per each recipe and introduce a yeast starter. It is important that not more than 1 pound (450 grams) of sugar per 5 quarts (4.5 liters) is used in addition to the fruit, unless a hydrometer is used, in which case, a starting gravity of 60-65 is desirable. All of the sugar is added at the start of the fermentation.

2. The yeast used should be a genuine champagne yeast. Visit your local winemaking supply store to see which ones are available.

3. Allow the wine to ferment in the usual manner, but rack it off its yeast as soon as the first tumultuous fermentation has subsided. (This will occur approximately when the hydrometer reading is 5 and ideally when a sugar test shows that 1½ percent to 1¾ percent sugar is remaining.)

4. The wine, now starting its secondary fermentation, is bottled in champagne bottles with special champagne corks bound on crosswise.

5. The bottles are kept for 8 days in a warm room (between 65°F, 17°C, and 70°F, 20°C) and are then moved to a cooler place (around 50°F, 12°C).

6. The bottles should be stored (preferably for 6 months at least) on a slight incline, cork down, and every day for a week or so, each bottle must be given an abrupt jerk an eighth of a turn to the left and right.

7. After at least a week of the *rémuage*, it will be found that the yeast sediment has settled on the cork, and a further wait is necessary merely to allow the wine to become thoroughly clear above. Cautious winemakers use a piece of blanket to hold the base of the bottle while carrying out this operation, in case a weakened bottle has been used.

8. When the wine is clear, the yeast sediment must be removed. This is a job requiring great care and some skill. The bottle is held at a steep angle, neck down, with one hand supporting it from beneath while the other hand removes the fastening and carefully eases out the cork. It will slide out slowly at first and then suddenly shoot out, carrying the yeast with it. Immediately the bottle must be turned upright and a thumb placed on top to force the carbon dioxide effervescence to die down. The last traces of yeast are then removed from the neck of the bottle with a finger and a small glass of brandy or brandy plus sugar syrup is added according to taste. The bottle is then re-stoppered and again fastened with stout string or wire.

(The actual dosage should be all brandy if a very dry champagne is required, or all sugar syrup if a sweet champagne is desired. Once you have made your first batch, you will quickly decide when drinking it whether to use the same dosage on future occasions or whether to make a mixture of brandy and sugar syrup.

9. The process can be made easier by employing a freezing bath of ice cubes and ordinary common salt, into which the necks of the bottles are placed for a while until a pellet of ice is seen to form in the neck of the bottle. This pellet of ice is forced out with the cork and less wine is lost than in the method described above. The sediment is also prevented from being disturbed during these operations because it is enclosed within the plug of ice in the neck of the bottle.

10. The bottles are then stored on their sides in a cool temperature for about a year before drinking.

Yet another method of removing the unwanted yeast is the use of a special cork. The cork is a special blister cork that collects the dead yeast while the bottle is inverted. Once the champagne is clear, the blister is wired off and the bottle chilled in a refrigerator.
The gas dissolves in the wine and a plastic champagne cork can then be used to seal the bottle.

Method 2

This involves making champagne from a completely finished wine. The two points to observe here are:

- The wine must not be above 8 percent alcohol (which again means a starting gravity of about 60).
- The wine must be perfectly clear. (To achieve this quickly, it is essential to have a balanced must and in some cases to use a pectic enzyme in the must.)

The cleared wine is drawn off into champagne bottles (ordinary ones may not be used as they cannot withstand the pressure) and a small glass of yeast culture is added. This has been prepared beforehand and is in full ferment when added.

The actual wine should be tested beforehand with a sugar testing kit (which should give a reading of ¼ percent or ½ percent sugar only).

The wine can then be primed with sugar syrup before being put in bottles and re-fermenting. For exact measurements, the following table will be of use. It should be remembered that the Clinitest sugar testing kit will only measure invert sugar, and while any original sugar added at the start of fermentation would have become invert sugar in the presence of yeast and acids, these kits will not measure very recently added sugar that has not yet been inverted.

To obtain about four atmospheres pressure, we require 1½ percent sugar, which is 0.5-0.6 ounces per quart (15-16 grams per liter) or 2.5 ounces per 5 quarts (70 grams per 4.5 liters).

Sugar remaining in the wine	Sugar to be added per 5 quarts (4.5 liters) before bottling
0	2½ oz. (70 g.)
¼%	2¼ oz. (60 g.)
½%	1¾ oz. (50 g.)
¾%	1½ oz. (40 g.)
1%	1 oz. (25 g.)
1¼%	½ oz. (15 g.)
1½%	¼ oz. (5 g.)
1¾%	None

Wines containing 2 percent or more sugar should not be used for champagne production.

The bottles are dealt with in exactly the same way as in Method 1 (from Step 5 onward).

Before continuing with some recipes, let us reiterate the safety precautions required:

1. Never make champagne without using a hydrometer and a sugar testing kit.
2. Not more than 1 lb. (450 g.) of sugar per 5 quarts (4.5 liters), in addition to that in the fruit (starting gravity of 60), should be used.
3. Use champagne bottles only.
4. When handling bottles, hold them in a piece of thick cloth and keep your face as far away from the bottles as possible.

Recipe 1
INGREDIENTS

- 4 lb. (1.8 kg.) green gooseberries
- 10 fl. oz. (280 ml.) white grape concentrate
- 10 fl. oz. (280 ml.) elderflowers or yellow rose petals (lightly pressed down only)
- ½ oz. (15 g.) pectic enzyme
- Yeast nutrient
- Champagne yeast
- Honey or sugar syrup to specific gravity 60
- Water to 5 quarts (4.5 liters)

METHOD

Place the gooseberries in a plastic bucket and bruise them well with a piece of wood. Add the flowers and pour over them 7.5 pints (3 liters) of boiling water. When cool, add the grape concentrate, yeast nutrient, pectic enzyme, and enough sugar syrup or honey syrup to produce a specific gravity of 60.

Add the yeast starter and ferment on the pulp for 3 days, after which, strain off the fermenting must from the pulp and continue fermentation in a glass jar under a fermentation lock. Then proceed as detailed in either Method 1 or 2.

Recipe 2
INGREDIENTS

- 1 lb. (450 g.) dried apricots
- 10 fl. oz. (280 ml.) white grape concentrate
- 10 fl. oz. (280 ml.) elderflowers or yellow rose petals
- ½ oz. (15 g.) malic acid
- Yeast nutrient
- ¼ oz. (10 g.) pectic enzyme
- Water to 5 quarts (4.5 liters)
- Honey or sugar syrup to specific gravity 60

METHOD

Place the apricots and flowers in a plastic bucket and pour 7.5 pints (3 liters) of boiling water over them. When cool, add the malic acid, yeast nutrient, and pectic enzyme, stir well, and adjust the specific gravity to 60 with sugar syrup or honey.

Add the yeast starter and ferment on the pulp for 2-3 days only, after which, strain off into a demijohn and continue fermentation. Then proceed as described in Method 1 or 2.

Recipe 3
INGREDIENTS

- 5 quarts (4.5 liters) pear juice (or 2.5 quarts (2.25 liters) each, pear and dessert apple juice)
- 10 fl. oz. (280 ml.) white grape concentrate
- 10 fl. oz. (280 ml.) elderflowers or yellow rose petals
- ¼ oz. (10 g.) pectic enzyme
- Yeast nutrients
- Champagne yeast

METHOD

Place all of the ingredients in a plastic bucket and mix thoroughly. Adjust the specific gravity to 60 with sugar, if too low, or with water, if too high, and add an active yeast starter. When fermentation is going well, transfer to a jar. Then, proceed as detailed in Method 1 or 2.

Recipe 4
INGREDIENTS
- 1 lb. (450 g.) elderberries
- 1 lb. (450 g.) raisins
- ½ oz. (15 g.) malic acid
- Yeast nutrient
- ¼ oz. (10 g.) pectic enzyme
- Water to 5 quarts (4.5 liters)
- Sugar syrup to specific gravity 60

METHOD
Place chopped raisins and crushed elderberries in a plastic bucket and pour 7.5 pints (3 liters) of boiling water over them. When cool, add the malic acid, yeast nutrient, and pectic enzyme. Stir well and adjust the specific gravity to 60 with sugar syrup.

Add the yeast starter (champagne, Burgundy, or Bordeaux) and ferment on the pulp for 3 days, after which, strain off into a demijohn jar and continue fermenting. Then proceed as described in Method 1 or 2.

Recipe 5
INGREDIENTS
- ½ lb. (225 g.) dried bilberries
- 10 fl. oz. (280 ml.) white grape concentrate
- ½ oz. (15 g.) malic acid
- Yeast nutrient
- ¼ oz. (10 g.) pectic enzyme
- Water to 5 quarts (4.5 liters)
- Honey or sugar syrup to specific gravity 60

METHOD
Place the bilberries and grape concentrate in a plastic bucket and pour 7.5 pints (3 liters) of boiling water over them. When cool, add the malic acid, yeast nutrient, and pectic enzyme. Stir well and adjust the specific gravity to 60 with honey or sugar syrup. Add an active burgundy yeast starter and ferment on the pulp for 4-5 days until a sufficient depth of color has been achieved, after which, strain off into a demijohn jar and continue fermentation. Then continue as in Method 1 or 2.

Chapter 11

LIQUEURS AND APERITIFS

What is a liqueur? The basic definition is that it is a sweetened and flavored alcoholic beverage obtained by the distillation or infusion of aromatic and/or fruit substances with potable spirit. The name *liqueur* conjures up notions of lush banquets just finishing with diners groaning contentedly over their Cointreau, or the lounge bars of fashionable London taverns where Green Chartreuse is sipped in oddly shaped glasses with one's little finger cocked. In actual fact, liqueurs have become so muddled with other drinks, it seems best to lump them all together at the start and sort them out alphabetically as we go.

In most wine catalogues, aperitifs and liqueurs will occupy different sections, and in some catalogues, other titles also appear, such as: fruit brandies, cups and bitters, or alcoholic cordials. Further confusion arises when such drinks as the familiar Egg Rip (*advocaat*) are found in the aperitif section of one catalogue and in the liqueur section of another. Pernod, the fiery heir of the now-banned absinthe, is an aperitif, but in view of its considerable alcoholic strength, it is often bought and drunk by many people as though it were a liqueur, even though it lacks the sweetness that is normal in a liqueur.

Easy to Make

However, sweet or dry, whether drunk before or after meals, or in one's bath, the fact emerges that any amateur winemaker can easily make liqueurs. It is just a matter of obtaining the correct flavoring essence (all sorts of which are now readily available), using a reasonably or even a poor homemade wine as a base to supply part of the alcohol, adding sugar syrup and a spirit, and you are there. In most cases, the liqueur or aperitif is ready for immediate drinking. At this point, however, let us issue a note of warning, just to clear the air.

Homemade liqueurs and aperitifs must not be sold. Also, some liqueurs such as Benedictine, Chartreuse, Grand Marnier, and Strega are proprietary names and in consequence, homemade liqueurs should not be labeled with these names.

NOT IDENTICAL

In the recipes that follow, it is not claimed that any of these will produce a product that is identical to the liqueurs described in the heading above the recipe.

Digressing for a moment, it is curious how touchy some makers of drinks are about any attempt on the part of the amateur to copy their products, even though no question of selling them is involved. There was a certain amount of prejudice against amateurs in the early days of the winemaking movement. Voices were even raised within the movement against the establishment of a National Committee in Britain, lest this centralization should invite legislation against amateur winemakers in Parliament, pressurized by the big commercial concerns.

In actual fact, the large wine companies in Britain, such as Grants of St. James, the Victoria Wine Company, and Harveys of Bristol have gone out of their way to be pleasant and friendly to amateur winemakers, giving lectures with splendid free samples. They knew what they were doing, for during the period from 1958-1963 when the amateur winemaking movement was mushrooming, clearances of wine through customs in Britain rose from 15 million gallons to 23 million gallons. This is an average increase of 10 percent per annum, considerably in excess of the 4 percent rise in productivity desired by the rest of the country's industries.

AMATEURS BOOST SALES

The truth of the matter is that if you make a wine or a liqueur that should bear some resemblance to a commercial article, you cannot resist heading off to buy a bottle of the real thing to see how well you have triumphed in your own efforts.

If liqueur making becomes popular in amateur circles, the sales of liqueurs will boom, as have the wine sales. It's not just what you drink yourself—for if you have something good, you let your friends taste it and they will acquire the taste for it, and so the gentle art of gracious tippling spreads throughout the whole community.

EXPERIENCING THE RANGE

You have to experience the vast range of flavors that exist in the world of liqueurs and aperitifs to appreciate what a fascinating territory exists for your exploring. One of the authors has (or rather had) a fair-sized collection of miniatures gathered from all over Europe. Miniatures seem to be a recognized form of present at Christmas and for birthdays to give amateur winemakers. Their attractive shapes and colors add an air of quality to the multitude of tiny bars that we possess in our wineries.

Not so long ago, on an impulse, with a few friends, it was decided to liquidate this collection and a most exciting exploration of this scintillating world of liqueurs took place over several evenings. The bottles still stand on the shelves above the bar, now alas filled with apricot wine only, but their memory lives on as one's glance wanders from bottle to bottle.

In the course of preparing this section, it was necessary to check on most of the recipes issued by the manufacturing companies supplying the essences. Indeed, in some cases four or five checks on the one recipe were made with different wines, strengths of spirit, and even different base spirits.

It would have taken the resources of a king to make a complete bottle for each experiment, and thus a laboratory method of preparing small samples had to be devised.

After a few initial failures, this technique proved so successful that it is possible, armed with a variety of essences, one or two bottles of basic wine, some sugar syrup, and half a bottle of Polish spirit to make glasses of liqueurs to order, so to speak. This laboratory method will be outlined in detail in a later section, as it may prove of value to wine guilds seeking their own individual guild liqueur without spending too much of the guild funds in the search for the right recipe.

We must admit that our recipes differ considerably in some cases from those advocated by the supplier of the essence. This is a case of our personal taste. We must also add that for some types of liqueurs, one supplier's essence was found to be greatly superior to another's. This too may be a question of personal taste. In the long run, quality will triumph, so, if you find that a liqueur is not quite up to your expectations, first try an alternative essence if one is available, and if that is still not successful, change your basic wine. In many cases, the change of essence will achieve the success you require.

BROWSING FOR ESSENCES

Essence-bottle browsing at your local supplier can become as fascinating a pastime as a mall filled with only bookstores would be to booklovers. In the course of browsing, you will come across a variety, including sherry, port, Madeira, Burgundy, gin, whiskey, and brandy (or *eau-de-vie*). Strictly speaking, these are intended for improving poor-flavored wines. The idea is that you make a wheat wine, say, add a little of the whiskey extract, and give the wine to your friends hoping they will think you have a secret still.

The gin flavors seem to have the greatest possibilities, we believe. There are still many unsolved problems in winemaking, and one of these is what to do with friends who are confirmed spirit drinkers. Now most gin drinkers do not drink it neat, but generally with water or bitter lemon. This dilution brings the strength down to about 35 proof. It should therefore be possible to make a wine of a fairly neutral and almost colorless nature, add to it some gin essence and possibly some citron essence, fortify it slightly by adding about 3 fluid ounces

(89 milliliters) of 140 proof spirit per bottle, and give it to friends who will think they are drinking gin and bitter lemon. The difficulty is finding the right ingredients, and so far we have not found the answer.

The whiskey flavor is also a difficult one to match and would require a grain wine base. Rum, however, offers a much greater chance of success because many people tend to drink it with orange. If you have some Seville orange wine that still has a little bite to it, try adding a little rum flavor to it—an interesting drink to end an evening.

Kits are also now available to make you own liqueurs. By adding a bottle of your favorite commercial spirit, you will end up with seven bottles at roughly a quarter of the price of commercial equivalents.

STRONG WINE BASE

Because most liqueurs and aperitifs range in strength from about 30 proof up to lone giants, such as Green Chartreuse (96 proof), it is important that a strong wine is used as a base.

We have assumed in these recipes that a wine of 28 proof is available. (That is 16 percent alcohol by volume and equals the strength of our strong wines.) What is more important is that the wine should normally not have too powerful a flavor of its own. There are nevertheless exceptions to this rule, for in the course of one experiment it was found that a powerfully flavored elderberry wine blended wonderfully with an orange essence to produce a new flavor that was neither elderberry nor orange.

By and large, however, rather dull uninteresting wines seem to be more suitable, and their main function in these cases is simply to provide part of the required alcohol. The question of the color of the wine is not important except for the purists. Liqueurs are as individual as their makers in the commercial field, and such liqueurs as Curacao appear in red, white, and even blue colors. The familiar Crème de Menthe is best known in its green form, but white and pink varieties also exist.

For most purposes, 140 proof Polish spirit is the best medium for fortification, because it is neutral in taste and so strong that it is well above the strength of the most powerful liqueurs (which in general range around 70 proof, the strength of whiskey, gin, rum, and brandy). Some of the lower-strength liqueurs and fruit brandies in the range 35-50 proof can be made with advantage with brandy, rum, or gin, but we suggest some initial experimentation with small quantities as described in the next section before full-scale production is attempted. It is unfortunate that the customs duty on Polish spirit raises its price, but half a bottle goes a long way, especially with the lower-strength liqueurs such as cherry brandy.

The sweetening syrup is made by heating 2 pounds (900 grams) of sugar with 20 fluid ounces (570 milliliters) of water, allowing it to boil for a few moments until the solution becomes quite clear and colorless. This syrup must, of course, be allowed to cool before being used.

PREPARING LIQUEURS

The basic method of preparing liqueurs and aperitifs is very simple. Measure the amount of Polish spirit required, add the essence, mix well, and pour it into the bottle. Then measure the amount of syrup required and pour this into the bottle too. Pour a little wine into the measure cup, swirling it around to wash the last traces of the spirit, essence, and syrup, and add it to the bottle. Finally, top off the bottle with more wine. The bottle should then be shaken well to mix the ingredients. The measuring cup should not be washed between additions, for it is essential that all traces of the essence eventually finish up in the bottle, most being added with the spirit, but traces with the syrup and wine.

Most liqueurs are ready to drink immediately after mixing, because they do not mature with age as wines do. The essential factor to ensure success is that all the ingredients should become intimately mixed. Only with the more delicately flavored liqueurs is there a slight advantage in leaving the liqueurs to stand for a week or two or even a month or so.

The following table gives the relative amounts in fluid ounces (milliliters) that will produce sample lots of 3 fluid ounces (80 milliliters) of liqueurs of various strengths. Because 3 fluid ounces (80 milliliters) is approximately one-tenth of a bottle, it is ample to allow four or five people to taste each liqueur sample.

Wine of 28 proof	Sugar syrup	Spirit of 140 proof	Final strength of liqueur
2 fl. oz. (56 ml.)	0.5 fl. oz. (15 ml.)	0.3 fl. oz. (9 ml.)	35 proof
1.75 fl. oz. (53 ml.)	0.5 fl. oz. (15 ml.)	0.4 fl. oz. (12 ml.)	40 proof
1.7 fl. oz. (50 ml.)	0.5 fl. oz. (15 ml.)	0.5 fl. oz. (15 ml.)	44 proof
1.6 fl. oz. (47 ml.)	0.5 fl. oz. (15 ml.)	0.6 fl. oz. (18 ml.)	48 proof
1.5 fl. oz. (44 ml.)	0.5 fl. oz. (15 ml.)	0.7 fl. oz. (21 ml.)	52 proof
1.4 fl. oz. (41 ml.)	0.5 fl. oz. (15 ml.)	0.8 fl. oz. (24 ml.)	56 proof
1.3 fl. oz. (38 ml.)	0.5 fl. oz. (15 ml.)	0.9 fl. oz. (27 ml.)	60 proof
1.2 fl. oz. (35 ml.)	0.5 fl. oz. (15 ml.)	1 fl. oz. (30 ml.)	64 proof
1.1 fl. oz. (32 ml.)	0.5 fl. oz. (15 ml.)	1.1 fl. oz. (32 ml.)	69 proof
1 fl. oz. (29 ml.)	0.5 fl. oz. (15 ml.)	1.2 fl. oz. (35 ml.)	73 proof
0.9 fl. oz. (26 ml.)	0.5 fl. oz. (15 ml.)	1.3 fl. oz. (38 ml.)	77 proof

In the lower-strength liqueurs (say 44 proof), a half bottle of 140 proof Polish spirit will serve for over twenty separate experiments with four or five people tasting each time, (a half bottle contains just under 13.5 fl. oz., 400 ml.).

We have maintained the syrup level as a constant in the above table, but this can be varied as explained later.

Because of the size of the quantities used, it is best to have two simple pieces of equipment: a graduated 1-milliliter pipette (eye-dropper type) and a 100-milliliter measuring cylinder. These two items will keep you from having to measure values like 0.3 fluid ounces.

TASTE TESTING

The initial part of each taste testing is simple. Let us suppose the tasting committee decides that, for a start, they are thinking in terms of a liqueur of about 56 proof. Wine is first poured into the measuring cylinder up to the 41-milliliter mark (see table). Then, 15 milliliters of sugar syrup are poured in, bringing it up to the 56-milliliter mark. Then, 24 milliliters of Polish spirit (140 proof) are poured in, as indicated by the table, bringing the level up to the 80-milliliter mark. All that has to be done now is to introduce the extract or essence, stir well, and drink.

The introduction of the flavorings needs a steady hand and a clear mind. There is nearly always someone with these qualities in every guild who is capable of handling a 1-milliliter graduated pipette accurately. The essences themselves are supplied in varying strengths according to the manufacturer. Because in these test samples we are making only one-tenth of a bottle of liqueur at a time, it is necessary to use only one-tenth the amount of extract.

A teaspoon holds 5 milliliters, so that wherever one teaspoon of essence is mentioned in a recipe, only 0.3 milliliters are required in these test samples. It is very much simpler to do than to describe. If, however, difficulty is experienced in obtaining three-tenths of a milliliter, or if a graduated 1-milliliter pipette is not easily obtainable, the ordinary 1-milliliter pipette (which has just the single 1-milliliter mark on it) can be used. Simply pour wine into the measuring cylinder up to the 30-milliliter mark, add the 1 milliliter of essence, and stir well. Then pour off 20 milliliters of this into some other container, and the 10 milliliters remaining will contain the one-teaspoon equivalent of essence per bottle. The wine is then made up to its original mark according to the table.

From these test samplings, a very good idea can be obtained of how the extracts blend with the different types of wine and it can be decided whether the sugar level is too high or low.

Once a satisfactory formula has been discovered and all the tasting committee sworn to secrecy, a full bottle can be made with accuracy.

Sometimes the tasting committee will deviate from the preceding table and arrive at a satisfactory formula, but not any longer be able to define the strength of the liqueur. This is easily arrived at in the following manner. Let us suppose that 20 milliliters wine, 10 milliliters of sugar syrup, and 20 milliliters of spirit produced the final liqueur. Simply multiply each item by its alcohol strength (including the sugar, which has a strength of zero) and divide by the total volume.

Volume multiplied by Strength		Total
Wine	20 ml. × 28 proof	560
Sugar	10 × 0	0
Spirit	20 × 140 proof	2800
	Total 50 ml.	3360

Divide the 3360 by 50 and the answer is 67 proof.

If the same proportions were used, but the wine was only 25 proof and ordinary gin (70 proof) was being used, the figures would be:

Wine	20 ml. × 25 proof	500
Sugar	10 × 0	0
Gin	20 × 70 proof	1400
	Total 50 ml	1900

1900 divided by 50 gives 38 proof strength of liqueur.

After that mathematical celebration, it is as well to return to recipes. All recipes are for one full wine bottle of liqueur.

Absinthe Group

These are spirit aperitifs, but the French drink them at all times of the day and night. Absinthe itself, a popular bit of still life in French Impressionist painting, is now banned because of its ill effects on health when drunk in quantity. Its heirs, Pernod, Pastis, Anice, Anise, Anesone, and Anisette do not have the stigma of absinthe. Indeed, if one has indigestion or mild stomach upsets, it is difficult to find a better cure than three glasses of Pernod sipped steadily over the course of an evening. The following recipes have a similar flavoring base.

Recipe 1
INGREDIENTS
- 12 fl. oz. (340 ml.) of 140 proof spirit
- 5 fl. oz. (150 ml.) sugar syrup
- One teaspoon Anise essence

METHOD
Top off the bottle with white wine of low flavor. This aperitif will be 77 proof.

Recipe 2
INGREDIENTS
- 11.5 fl. oz. (360 ml.) of 140 proof Polish spirit
- 5 fl. oz. (150 ml.) sugar syrup
- 2 teaspoons Anisette extract

METHOD
Top off the bottle with white wine. This aperitif will be 73 proof. A slightly drier aperitif can be made using only 3 fl. oz. (90 ml.) of sugar syrup, and in this case, only one teaspoon of essence is normally required.

Recipe 3
INGREDIENTS
- 10.5 fl. oz. (330 ml.) of 140 proof Polish spirit
- 4 fl. oz. (120 ml.) sugar syrup
- 1 teaspoon Anisette essence

METHOD
Top off the bottle with white wine. This aperitif will be 70 proof.

Arack

During war, the one spirit forbidden to the British troops was *arack* (also known as *araq, ouzo*, and about two hundred other local names, including a few by courtesy of the British army). It was said to be bad for their health, but after a dozen forbidden *aracks*, it was generally the local population whose health tended to be put in jeopardy by the belligerence engendered by this fiery spirit. Modern *arack* on sale in Britain is a refined thing rated as magnificent by many people. The following recipes tend to approach the real thing.

Recipe 1
INGREDIENTS
- 11.5 fl. oz. (360 ml.) of 140 proof spirit
- 5 fl. oz. (150 ml.) sugar spirit
- 5 fl. oz. (150 ml.) whiskey
- 2 teaspoons Anisette extract

METHOD
Top off with a white wine (preferably a grain wine). This is 83 proof.

Recipe 2
INGREDIENTS
- 11.5 fl. oz. (360 ml.) of 140 proof spirit
- 5 fl. oz. (150 ml.) sugar syrup
- 1 teaspoon Anise essence

METHOD
Top off with Irish whiskey. This powerful concoction (86 proof) needs to be treated with considerable respect.

Advocaat

In wine merchants' catalogues, the following recipe always seems to be called an *advocaat* in the liqueur section and Egg Flip in the cocktail section. In the British army, it was called eggnog, and we are indebted to Bill Gregory for the recipe, which he has made in the Warrant Officers' Messes of Austria, Burma, and elsewhere in the Orient. It is an excellent pick-me-up for invalids and said to be beloved by duchesses.

INGREDIENTS
- The yolks of 3 large eggs
- 4 fl. oz. (120 ml.) sugar syrup
- 6 fl. oz. (180 ml.) gin or brandy
- Vanilla essence to taste
- Evaporated milk as required

METHOD
Chill all the ingredients in the refrigerator if possible. Beat the egg yolks well, and then add the sugar syrup, gin or brandy, and a little of the evaporated milk (say 4 fl. oz., 120 ml.). Continue beating until all are well blended. The ideal consistency of this liqueur is that it should only just pour, and enough additional evaporated milk should be beaten in to achieve this consistency. The amount required largely depends on the size of the eggs used. Finally, add the vanilla essence to taste.

Apricot Brandy

We have always been scrupulously honest with our readers, never pandering to popular appeal or covering up our differences or failures, and we must admit that here we ran into difficulties when first making test liqueurs of the apricot brandy type.

It seems to us that apricot wine would make an excellent base for apricot brandy, but apparently this is not necessarily so, and a scruffy old banana wine proved a much better base.

Recipe 1
INGREDIENTS
- 8 fl. oz. (240 ml.) of 140 proof spirit
- 5 fl. oz. (150 ml.) sugar syrup
- 2 teaspoons apricot brandy extract

METHOD
Top off with a white wine. This is 56 proof.

Recipe 2

- 9 fl. oz. (270 ml.) of 140 proof spirit
- 8 fl. oz. (240 ml.) sugar syrup
- 2 teaspoons apricot brandy extract

METHOD
Top off with white wine. This is 57 proof and represents the sweeter version of apricot brandy.

Recipe 3
INGREDIENTS

- 7 fl. oz. (210 ml.) of 140 proof spirit
- 3 fl. oz. (90 ml.) sugar syrup
- 1 teaspoon apricot brandy essence

METHOD
Top off with white wine. This is 54 proof and is much drier than the other versions. It can in fact be used as an aperitif.

Benedictine

This magnificent herb-based liqueur, another great product of the Benedictine monks, is very well known. The familiar bottles bear the letters D.O.M., which stand for *deo optimo maximo*, to God, the most good, the most great, a motto worthy of Benedictine, because it is probably one of the oldest of liqueurs, being made originally at the now ruined Abbey of Fécamp in Normandy.

It is one of the few liqueurs that has never really been successfully copied, for its flavors are very subtle. The following recipe, although producing a very fine liqueur, falls short of the magnificence of Benedictine. If you don't believe us, go out and buy a bottle. Perhaps you can do better, in which case we shall be glad to hear from you.

Recipe 1
INGREDIENTS

- 11.5 fl. oz. (360 ml.) of 140 proof spirit
- 5 fl. oz. (150 ml.) sugar syrup
- 2-3 teaspoons Reverendine extract

METHOD
Use a well-balanced smooth golden wine to top off the bottle. This is 73 proof.

Recipe 2
INGREDIENTS

- 11.5 fl. oz. (360 ml.) 140 proof spirit
- 4 fl. oz. (120 ml.) sugar syrup
- 1-2 teaspoons Benedictine essence

METHOD
Use a well-balanced smooth golden wine to top off the bottle. This is 74 proof.

Recipe 3
INGREDIENTS

- 11.5 fl. oz. (360 ml.) of 140 proof spirit
- 6 fl. oz. (180 ml.) sugar syrup
- 1 teaspoon Benedictine essence

METHOD
Use a well-balanced smooth golden wine to top off the bottle. This is 72 proof.

Chartreuse

This is the Queen of Liqueurs (the kingship generally being attributed to Benedictine), and like most women of character, it has subtlety, fire, enigma, and passion in its makeup. It was originally made by the Carthusian monks in the monastery of La Grande Chartreuse near Grenoble, but when the monks were expelled from France, they carried their secret with them to Spain and acquired a distillery near Tarragona. Today it is made both in France and Spain, but the Spanish product is mainly reserved for Latin American countries.

Chartreuse has a most complicated herb base, including angelica, balm leaves, hyssop, orange peel, and many other ingredients. It is made in three types: green at 96 proof, yellow at 75 proof, and a white variety that is stronger than the green, called Elixir, which can be difficult to find. We believe we must repeat the legendary story of the little Carthusian monk, who, when asked the secret of monastic happiness, replied with a twinkling eye, "One third green and two thirds yellow."

Recipe 1
INGREDIENTS

- 16 fl. oz. (510 ml.) of 140 proof spirit
- 7 fl. oz. (210 ml.) sugar syrup
- 2 teaspoons Green Convent extract

METHOD
Top off with white wine. This is 92 proof and may require sweetening further according to taste.

Recipe 2
INGREDIENTS

- 11.5 fl. oz. (360 ml.) of 140 proof spirit
- 6 fl. oz. (180 ml.) sugar syrup
- 1 small tablespoon mixed herbs

METHOD

The spirit and 8 fl. oz. (240 ml.) of a golden-colored wine are placed in a container and the herbs are tied in a muslin bag and immersed in this mixture for 4 days, after which they are pressed and the mixture is poured into a bottle. The sugar syrup is then added and if necessary, a golden-colored wine may be used to fill the bottle. If a golden wine is not available, yellow food coloring can be used to produce the true yellow liqueur.

Recipe 3
INGREDIENTS

- 12 fl. oz. (390 ml.) of 140 proof spirit
- 8 fl. oz. (240 ml.) sugar syrup
- 2-3 teaspoons Convent Yellow extract

METHOD

Top off with a golden wine. This is 75 proof.

Cherry Brandy

There are many fruit brandies, some made by distilling a fruit wine (i.e., Calvados distilled from cider) and others by simply soaking fruit in brandy. None of these have gained the popularity that is held by cherry brandy in Britain (even before the youthful Prince of Wales felt the long arm of the law descend on him in 1963 while enjoying a quiet tipple). It is one of the cheapest liqueurs to make, and one that is unbelievably close to the original. Well-matured elderberry wine (having lost its initial harshness) makes a splendid base for this liqueur. Cherry wine is also suitable, provided it has been made from deep-colored fruit.

There are two main types of cherry brandy on the market. One is full-bodied and lush, similar to the first two following recipes, and the other is full-bodied, but fruity, more like the third following recipe.

Recipe 1
INGREDIENTS

- 5 fl. oz. (150 ml.) of 140 proof spirit
- 5 fl. oz. (150 ml.) sugar syrup
- 1 teaspoon cherry brandy essence

METHOD

Top off with elderberry, red cherry, or bilberry wine. This is 44 proof.

Recipe 2
INGREDIENTS

- 5 fl. oz. (150 ml.) 140 proof spirit
- 5 fl. oz. (150 ml.) sugar syrup
- 1-2 teaspoons cherry brandy essence

METHOD

Top off with a red grape concentrate wine. This is 44 proof. It is best with this recipe to add only 1 teaspoon of the essence at first, mix well and taste, and then add the second teaspoonful only if additional flavor is required.

Recipe 3
INGREDIENTS

- 5 fl. oz. (150 ml.) of 140 proof spirit
- 5 fl. oz. (150 ml.) sugar syrup
- 2 teaspoons cherry brandy extract
- ½ teaspoon (2 ml.) citric acid

METHOD

Top off with a red wine, preferably elderberry. Add the citric acid. This is 44 proof.

Recipe 4

Take a jam jar and fill it with dark red cherries, which must be completely free of mold, bruises, or any form of decay. Each cherry is pierced with a fork several times before being dropped into the jar. Add 3 oz. (90 g.) of finely granulated white sugar and top off the jar with cheap brandy. Cover the jar with a polyethylene cover held in place by an elastic band and leave for 6 months, after which it can be strained through muslin and is ready for drinking. In some cases, a little additional sugar syrup may be needed according to taste.

This is a method that can be used, of course, for other fruits, such as sloes, damsons, prunes, or dates, and one can experiment with the home production of liqueurs in almost endless varieties and combinations. The high concentration of sugar and alcohol will prohibit fermentation, and all one is really doing is flavoring the chosen alcohol—it is worth experimenting, too, with vodka (which is itself tasteless) and gin—with the particular fruit or fruits employed. The method is extremely simple, if a little expensive.

Cherry Liqueurs

We have already mentioned cherry brandy, but there are a great many cherry-based liqueurs, and many of them do not taste of cherries so much as cherry pits, which give a flavor rather akin to almonds. Kirsch, Maraschino, and Ratafia are three of the best-known liqueurs in this category, but there are countless others, especially in Central Europe.

Recipe 1
INGREDIENTS

- 12 fl. oz. (390 ml.) 140 proof spirit
- 7 fl. oz. (210 ml.) sugar syrup
- 1 teaspoon Kirsch essence

METHOD

Top off with white wine. This is 75 proof.

Recipe 2
INGREDIENTS
- 9 fl. oz. (270 ml.) of 140 proof spirit
- 5 fl. oz. (150 ml.) sugar syrup
- 2 teaspoons Kirsch extract

METHOD
Top off with white wine. This is 60 proof.

Recipe 3
INGREDIENTS
- 8 fl. oz. (240 ml.) of 140 proof spirit
- 6 fl. oz. (180 ml.) sugar syrup
- 1-2 teaspoons Kirsch essence

METHOD
Top off with white wine. This is 55 proof. The addition of the essence can be made gradually until one's palate is satisfied.

Recipe 4
INGREDIENTS
- 9 fl. oz. (270 ml.) of 140 proof spirit
- 6 fl. oz. (180 ml.) sugar syrup
- 1 teaspoon Maraschino essence

METHOD
Top off with white wine. This is 60 proof.

Cocoa

Moving into realms domestic, we may as well include a couple of recipes with a cocoa flavor. The well-known liqueur in this range is called Crème de Cacao. It is very much an acquired taste.

Recipe 1
INGREDIENTS
- 6 fl. oz. (180 ml.) of 140 proof spirit
- 10 fl. oz. (300 ml.) sugar syrup
- 1-2 teaspoons Cacao extract

METHOD
Top off with any wine. This is 43 proof.

Recipe 2
INGREDIENTS
- 5 fl. oz. (150 ml.) of 140 proof spirit
- 5 fl. oz. (150 ml.) sugar syrup
- 1 teaspoon Cacao essence

METHOD
Top off with any wine. This is 43 proof.

Coffee Rum

While we are catering more for the female palate, it is as well to mention the range of coffee liqueurs, such as Tia Maria, Kahlua, etc. Drinks like these are quite easily made and we give a couple of recipes with a rum base that seems to blend itself well with coffee.

Recipe 1
Make 10 fl. oz. (280 ml.) of black coffee using a good blend of freshly ground coffee. While it is hot, dissolve ½ lb. (225 g.) of sugar in it. When it is cool, pour it into a wine bottle, straining it through a piece of muslin, and top off the bottle with rum. The flavor can be enhanced with 1 teaspoon coffee rum flavor. This is 33 proof.

Recipe 2
INGREDIENTS
- 4 fl. oz. (120 ml.) of 140 proof spirit
- 9 fl. oz. (270 ml.) sugar syrup
- 1 teaspoon coffee rum essence

METHOD
Top off with parsnip wine. This is 35 proof.

Crème de Menthe

It is puzzling why Crème de Menthe is so popular. It tastes of chewing gum, or alternatively toothpaste, and the flavor stays in the mouth for hours. Ladies seem to adore it, and children (if they can get their hands on it when one's back is turned) like it even more. However, if you take to Crème de Menthe, we appended some low-strength recipes.

Recipe 1
INGREDIENTS
- 3 fl. oz. (90 ml.) of 140 proof spirit
- 5 fl. oz. (150 ml.) sugar syrup
- 1-2 teaspoons green mint extract

METHOD
Top off with a table wine. This is 35 proof.

Recipe 2
INGREDIENTS
- 4 fl. oz. (120 ml.) of 140 proof spirit
- 7 fl. oz. (210 ml.) sugar syrup
- 1 teaspoon Crème de Menthe flavor

METHOD
Top off with a table wine. This is 37 proof.

Recipe 3
INGREDIENTS
- 4 fl. oz. (120 ml.) of 140 proof spirit
- 9 fl. oz. (270 ml.) sugar syrup
- 1-2 teaspoons white mint extract

METHOD
Top off with white table wine. This is 35 proof.

Recipe 4
INGREDIENTS
- 3 fl. oz. (90 ml.) of 140 proof spirit
- 6 fl. oz. (180 ml.) sugar syrup
- 1 teaspoon Crème de Menthe essence

METHOD
Top off with white wine. This is 34 proof.

Drambuie

This is undoubtedly our finest liqueur. It is made in the Isle of Skye and is also called Prince Charles Edward's Liqueur. We would place it as the equal of Benedictine and Chartreuse. Like them it is an herb-based liqueur (herbs blended with honey and liqueur whiskey). Tradition says it was originally made for bonnie Prince Charlie and that when he was rescued from pursuers, with few belongings other than the clothes he wore, his gratitude to his rescuers was such that he gave them the most precious thing he had, the secret recipe for his own liqueur. They have been making it ever since, and it is now an established favorite.

INGREDIENTS

- 10.5 fl. oz. (330 ml.) of 140 proof spirit
- 5 fl. oz. (150 ml.) sugar syrup
- 1 teaspoon honey smoke flavor

METHOD

Top off with a full-bodied white wine (a grain wine if possible). This is 69 proof.

Kummel

The potato is a much-maligned vegetable. We must confess, as winemakers, that neither of the authors has ever made potato wine. In Ireland, of course, they make it and then distil it into a fiery spirit called *poteen* (pronounced *potcheen*). When you drink it new, you can go up five flights without ever touching the stairway. In Europe, they also distil potato wine and then flavor it with caraway seeds. The result is Kummel—just the thing for an English winter, but rather surprisingly, it is still not popular.

Recipe 1

INGREDIENTS

- 10.5 fl. oz. (330 ml.) of 140 proof spirit
- 5 fl. oz. (150 ml.) sugar syrup
- 2 teaspoons Kummel extract

METHOD

Top off with low-flavored white wine. This is 69 proof.

Recipe 2

INGREDIENTS

- 9 fl. oz. (270 ml.) of 140 proof spirit
- 4 fl. oz. (120 ml.) sugar syrup
- 1 teaspoon Kummel essence

METHOD

Top off with white wine. This is 62 proof.

Goldwasser and Silberwasser

Centuries ago, when Europe was riddled with dreadful infections such as the bubonic plague, gold, and to a lesser extent, silver, became the cure-all of the most unlikely conditions. Medicinal liqueurs were made containing gold leaf and silver leaf, and the most famous of these, *Goldwasser de Lachs*, was made in Danzig and is still obtainable today. Silver water (*Silberwasser*) is not now sold in Britain, but *Goldwasser* has considerable appeal, though the tiny flecks of gold leaf are added purely for their attractiveness. *Goldwasser* has an aniseed base, and to this extent it resembles Pernod. You can find a Danzig extract that is complete with its gold leaf, and this liqueur generally proves fascinating to people when they first make its acquaintance.

INGREDIENTS

- 10.5 fl. oz. (330 ml.) of 140 proof spirit
- 4 fl. oz. (120 ml.) sugar syrup
- 1 bottle Danzig essence

METHOD
Top off with as colorless a wine as possible. This is 70 proof.

Orange Liqueurs

Wherever oranges are grown, with all their variations, tangerines, mandarins, naartjies, clementines, etc., liqueurs have been made using the peel of the fruit as a flavoring. Quite apart from the varieties of fruit, there are degrees of ripeness and changes of basic spirit. As a result, there is a whole range of liqueurs that are collectively known as curacaos. They come in all colors—red, blue, white, pink, and green—the coloring being mostly vegetable dyes (which incidentally are available to amateur winemakers through their usual suppliers).

Here and there, a curacao has achieved such greatness that its name is greater than curacao itself. Cointreau and Grand Marnier are two such names, while the South African liqueur Van der Hum (translated as "What's-his-name") is another, but with a rum flavor in addition to the fruit flavor. Because curacaos are among the easiest liqueurs to make successfully, and liqueurs that, with a variation of the basic wine, achieve new and interesting flavors, we can recommend these as a good starting point, and include a number of recipes.

Recipe 1
INGREDIENTS

- 7 fl. oz. (210 ml.) of 140 proof spirit
- 5 fl. oz. (150 ml.) sugar syrup
- 1 teaspoon curacao flavor

Recipe 2
INGREDIENTS
- 8 fl. oz. (240 ml.) of 140 proof spirit
- 7 fl. oz. (210 ml.) sugar syrup
- 1 teaspoon curacao essence

METHOD
Top off with white wine. This is 54 proof.

Recipe 3
Carefully grate the peel of an unripe orange (an orange with small patches of green, because a completely unripe one is not likely to be found). Soak the peel in 11.5 fl. oz. (360 ml.) of 140 proof spirit for 2 days. Strain off and add 5 fl. oz. (150 ml.) of sugar syrup and top off with a fairly low-flavored wine, such as carrot, birch sap, or vine leaf. Mix well and taste. At this stage, add up to 2 teaspoons of orange flavor little by little and tasting between additions. This produces a very full-flavored liqueur of about 73 proof.

Recipe 4
INGREDIENTS
- 9 fl. oz. (270 ml.) of 140 proof spirit
- 5 fl. oz. (150 ml.) sugar syrup
- 2-3 teaspoons curacao extract

METHOD
Top off with elderflower wine. This is 60 proof.

Recipe 5
INGREDIENTS
- 5 fl. oz. (150 ml.) of 140 proof spirit
- 5 fl. oz. (150 ml.) sugar syrup
- 2-3 teaspoons orange extract

METHOD
Top off with orange or lemon wine. This is 44 proof.

Recipe 6
INGREDIENTS
- 6 fl. oz. (180 ml.) of 140 proof spirit
- 2 fl. oz. (60 ml.) sugar syrup
- 1 teaspoon orange essence

METHOD
Top off with wine made from Seville oranges. This is 51 proof and is intended as an aperitif.

Recipe 7

INGREDIENTS

- 10 fl. oz. (300 ml.) of 140 proof spirit
- 4 fl. oz. (120 ml.) sugar syrup
- 1-2 teaspoons mandarin extract

METHOD

Top off with elderberry wine. This is 62 proof and particularly pleased our palate.

Peach Brandy

This liqueur is, in our opinion, better than cherry brandy, yet it has never acquired the same following.

INGREDIENTS

- 9 fl. oz. (270 ml.) of 140 proof spirit
- 7 fl. oz. (210 ml.) sugar syrup
- 2-3 teaspoons peach brandy extract

METHOD

Top off with white wine (preferably a peach wine). This is 58 proof.

Pineapple

Very occasionally in some wine merchants' catalogues, there appears the liqueur Crème d'Ananas, a pineapple-flavored alcoholic cordial. It is not very popular as a cordial, but with a little sugar only, it makes an attractive liqueur, for the flavor blends very well with most of our white wines.

INGREDIENTS

- 3 fl. oz. (90 ml.) of 140 proof spirit
- 4 fl. oz. (120 ml.) sugar syrup
- 3 teaspoons Ananas extract

METHOD

Top off with white wine. This is 36 proof.

Plum

If you ever go to what was once Yugoslavia, they give you Slivovitz to drink (local stuff, which is anything up to 110 proof). If you are inexperienced, you generally go blue in the face and the friendly Serbs thump you on the back until you recover, laughing merrily throughout. Thereafter, you are a welcome guest. Slivovitz is plum brandy, and while other blander plum brandies are made elsewhere in the world (Prunelle, Mirabelle, Quetsch, etc.) some of which taste of plums and some more of almonds, Slivovitz is the one that spoken of in awe.

Recipe 1
INGREDIENTS
- 10.5 fl. oz. (330 ml.) of 140 proof spirit
- 5 fl. oz. (150 ml.) sugar syrup
- 2-3 teaspoons Prunelle extract

METHOD
Top off with wine (a plum or damson if you have it). This is 69 proof.

Recipe 2
INGREDIENTS
- 10.5 fl. oz. (330 ml.) of 140 proof spirit
- 7 fl. oz. (210 ml.) sugar syrup
- 2-3 teaspoon Prunelle extract

METHOD
Top off with light red wine. This is 66 proof. If, in this recipe and the previous one, the sugar is lowered to only 1 or 2 fl. oz. (30-60 ml.) and additional wine is used, something approaching a mild form of Slivovitz will result. It can be used as an excellent aperitif.

Pomegranate

There is an alcoholic cordial called grenadine that has a pomegranate base. Alcoholic cordials were very popular about a hundred years ago, but their low alcohol strength and over sweetness make them rather unpopular today. Nevertheless, grenadine has a most interesting flavor, and one that blends very well with a young fruity wine, and although this extract was originally produced to improve indifferent wines, it can be made into a very pleasant fruit brandy.

Recipe 1
INGREDIENTS
- 5 fl. oz. (150 ml.) of 140 proof spirit
- 5 fl. oz. (150 ml.) sugar syrup
- 2-3 teaspoons grenadine extract

METHOD
Top off with any fruit wine. This is 44 proof.

Recipe 2
INGREDIENTS
- 6 fl. oz. (180 ml.) of 140 proof spirit
- 7 fl. oz. (210 ml.) sugar syrup
- 1 teaspoon grenadine essence
- ½ teaspoon (2 g.) citric acid

METHOD
Top off with any wine. This is 45 proof.

Punch

Most people think of punch as a festive drink, but not as a liqueur. In actual fact, there are several liqueurs called punch. In the west of Britain, there is a liqueur made at Burnham-on-Sea called Olde Exmoor Punch. It is a delightful refreshing liqueur and ought to be much more popular.

INGREDIENTS
- 4 fl. oz. (120 ml.) lime juice
- 14 fl. oz. (450 ml.) brandy
- 7 fl. oz. (210 ml.) rum
- 3 teaspoons punch extract

METHOD
The extract should be added a little at a time until the required taste has been achieved. This is 58 proof.

Sloe Gin

For this one recipe we return to the ancient tradition of Britain and give a method known to our grandmothers and theirs before them.

Fill a jar with fresh ripe sloes (discarding any that show signs of damage or mold). Each sloe must be pricked a few times with a fork. Add 10 oz. (300 g.) of sugar to every 1 lb. (450 g.) of sloes. Leave for 10 days and then fill the jar up with gin. The jar should then be sealed for 2-3 months, and inverted from time to time, after which the liquor should be strained off and bottled.

Strega

This is the proprietary name of a famous Italian liqueur. *Strega* means "witch," for it is said to have a bewitching effect and rates high in the armory of love potions. Like many of the highest-ranking liqueurs, it is herb-based, and its exact composition is a closely guarded secret.

Take a large jam jar or similar container, capable of holding a bottle of wine, and put into it 10 fl. oz. (300 ml.) of white wine and 11.5 fl. oz. (360 ml.) of 140 proof spirit. Take 2 small tablespoons (slightly below level) of mixed herbs, tied in a small muslin bag, and infuse this in the mixture for 4 days. Press out, pour into the bottle, and top off with 5-6 fl. oz. (150 ml.) of sugar syrup to taste. A slight haze may on occasion be apparent. This can be removed by fining or filtering, or by leaving the liqueur to clear naturally.

Vermouth

When one of the authors was in Palestine during World War II, he used to assist in the vineyard and in the winery of the French Trappist monastery of Latrun. It was a pleasant way of passing weekends and leaves. The quality of wine was excellent, and a great deal was discovered about the importance of cleanliness in the winery and the endless battle that has to be fought against hostile bacteria.

The quality of the monks' wine was such that orders came from officers' messes as far away as Egypt, Syria, and Lebanon. Now the Trappists, as unpaid workers laboring from first light to dusk, attempted to do everything to perfection, purely for the greater glory of God. Most of the surplus wealth derived from wine sales was spent on alleviating the poverty among the local people. Nevertheless, even with such dedication, the attempt to increase output to cope with the apparent endless thirst of the British resulted in an occasional small batch of wine being spoiled. The spoilage might have consisted of a mild bacterial infection, but more commonly arose from oxidation. These wines were converted into vermouth and were generally drunk with gin.

The origin of the word vermouth is in the principal herb used to flavor these wines, namely wormwood. Wormwood (*Artemisia absinthium*) has been valued medicinally for hundreds of years for its anthelmintic value and as a general tonic for weak stomachs. It is also a very good preservative, equal to hops, and has therefore been added to meads, cordials, and wines for centuries. It is a very bitter herb, and other herbs have been added to it to modify its flavor. It is the combination of these that form the basis of vermouth. Other herbs used are balm, yarrow, chamomile, cloves, nutmeg, coriander, gentian, and thyme.

For most winemakers, it is fortunate that many of our main winemaking suppliers supply packets of vermouth herbs for both French and Italian vermouth. The basic process is to make a small cotton bag, fill it with the herbs, and then to attach a piece of cotton to it and to poke the bag through the opening of a gallon jar, holding the cotton in place with the bung. Every day for a few days the bag is swirled around the wine in the jar until enough flavor has been extracted, after which the bag is removed and wine allowed to mature slightly and clear. This latter clarification process is the most difficult, because many of the herbs used impart a slight moonstone type of haze, which is very difficult to dispose of except by filtration.

To combat this, it is preferable to stuff one's cotton bag of herbs into a medicine bottle and to pour on a mixture of one's strongest wine with a miniature bottle of vodka or brandy. The extraction process is much quicker than in the liqueur itself, taking perhaps 2 days only at normal temperatures, following which the essence is decanted off into the wine with little risk of haze.

Winemakers will have realized the principal problem is achieving the degree of flavor desired. This is slightly complicated by the flavor of the wine being treated and the fact that the vermouth flavor diminishes with time. We have found that a vermouth kept for 2 years had lost so much of its original flavor as to be no longer recognizable as vermouth. It is better, therefore, to slightly over-flavor and to store the wine in the bottle for a couple of months before drinking it. If by some chance excessive vermouth flavor has been imparted, this is easily remedied by diluting the flavor with more wine.

In conclusion, while the purpose of this chapter is to provide a drinkable wine, mainly as an aperitif, from what would otherwise be a winemaker's failure, there is a small band of vermouth connoisseurs in the world who will no doubt concoct their own mixtures of herbs for infusion. We would remind these winemakers that commercial vermouths are generally around 18-20 percent alcohol by volume (roughly 30-35 proof) so that any worthy achievement in this field could be crowned by a little judicious fortification.

We hope that this little adventure into the world of liqueurs and aperitifs will have proved interesting, and that you will venture further yourselves. It is such an individual world that you will be doing more or less what your ancestors did hundreds of years back. Trial and error is the essence of this art. What few rules there are, have been described. Some of the essences can be blended themselves with advantage, but this leap in the dark is your privilege. Your own wines provide another variable element, so that you may stumble on some new flavor or bouquet. We wish you good luck in your attempts.

INDEX

A
Absinthe
  Recipes
    Recipe 1, 107-108
    Recipe 2, 108
    Recipe 3, 108
    Recipe 4, 108
    Recipe 5, 108
Acidity, role in winemaking, 19
Advocaat, making, 109
Alcohol level, determining,
  how to, 18
Alsatian wine
  Recipes
    Recipe 10, 47
Apricot Brandy, recipes, 109-110

B
Benedictine
  Recipes
    Recipe 1, 110
    Recipe 2, 110
    Recipe 3, 111

C
Casks, use of, warning, 59
Champagne and
  Sparkling Wines
    about, 90, 92
    methods, 90
    adapting for amateurs
      Method 1, 95-96
      Method 2, 97
    adding carbon dioxide, 93
    bottle fermentation, 93-94
    daily twist, 94-95
    Dom Perignon, 92-93
    sugar and gas pressure, 94
    tank fermentation, 93
  Recipes
    Recipe 1, 98
    Recipe 2, 98
    Recipe 3, 98
    Recipe 4, 99
    Recipe 5, 99
Chartreuse
  Recipes
    Recipe 1, 111
    Recipe 2, 111-112
    Recipe 3, 112
Cherry Brandy
  Recipes
    Recipe 1, 112
    Recipe 2, 112-113

Recipe 3, 113
Recipe 4, 113
Cherry Liqueur
  Recipes
    Recipe 1, 113
    Recipe 2, 114
    Recipe 3, 114
    Recipe 4, 114
Chianti, 68-70
  Basic method, 70-71
  Recipes
    Recipe 1 (old-style), 71
    Recipe 2 (old style), 72
    Recipe 3 (new style), 72
    Recipe 4 (new style), 72
    Recipe 5 (old style), 72-73
    Recipe 6 (new style), 73
Cocoa
  Recipes
    Recipe 1, 114
    Recipe 2, 115
Coffee Rum
  Recipes
    Recipe 1, 115
    Recipe 2, 115

D
Drambuie
  Recipe, 116-117

G
Goldwasser
  Recipe, 117

H
Homemade wine
  equipment, 13
  how good, 9
  how to make, 11-12
  ingredients, 12
  ordinary, how to make, 13-16
  quality, 9
Hocks
  Recipes
    Recipe 1, 44
    Recipe 2, 44
    Recipe 6, 45
    Recipe 7, 46
    Recipe 8, 46-47
    Recipe 9. 47
Hydrometer, 16
  table, 17

K
Kummel
  Recipes
    Recipe 1, 117
    Recipe 2, 117

L
Liebfraumilch
  Recipe, 45
Liqueurs and aperitifs, 100-105

M
Madeira
  Basic Method, 77
  Producing, 75-76
  Recipes
    Recipe 1 (Sercial or
      Verdelho), 77
    Recipe 2 (Sercial or
      Verdelho), 77-78
    Recipe 3 (Sercial or
      Verdelho), 78
    Recipe 4 (Sercial or
      Verdelho), 7
    Recipe 5 (Sercial or
      Verdelho), 79
    Recipe 6 (Sercial or
      Verdelho), 79
    Recipe 7 (Bual or
      Malmsey), 80
    Recipe 8 (Bual or
      Malmsey), 80
    Recipe 9 (Bual or
      Malmsey), 80-81
    Recipe 10 (Bual or
      Malmsey), 81
    Recipe 11 (Bual or
      Malmsey), 81
Moselles
  Alcohol volume table, 42
  Making, basic method, 43
  Recipes
    Recipe 3, 44-45
    Recipe 5, 45

O
Orange Liqueur
  Recipes
    Recipe 1, 118-119
    Recipe 2, 119
    Recipe 3, 119
    Recipe 4, 119
    Recipe 5, 119
    Recipe 6, 119
    Recipe 7, 119

Index

P
Peach Brandy
  Recipe, 120
Pineapple Cordial
  Recipe for, 120
Plum
  Recipes
    Recipe 1, 122
    Recipe 2, 121
Pomegranate
  Recipes
    Recipe 1, 121-122
    Recipe 2, 122
Port
  Making, basic method, 34-35
  Recipes
    Recipe 1, 35
    Recipe 2, 35
    Recipe 3, 35-36
    Recipe 4, 36
    Recipe 5, 36
    Recipe 6, 36-37
    Recipe 7, 37
    Recipe 8, 37
    Recipe 9, 38
    Recipe 10, 38
    Recipe 11, 39
    Recipe 12, 39
Punch
  Recipe for, 122

R
Red wines
  Basic method, 52
  Recipes
    Recipe 1, 52-53
    Recipe 2, 53
    Recipe 4, 53-54
    Recipe 5, 54
    Recipe 7, 55
  Types
    Beaujolais, 50
    Bordeaux, 50-51
    Claret, 51-52
      Recipe 3, 53
      Recipe 6, 54
Rosé
  about, 82-84
  best, 84
  enzyme use, 86

fermentation care, 85
making, basic method, 86
pink problem, 85
racking caution, 85
Recipes
  Recipe 1, 86
  Recipe 2, 87
  Recipe 3, 87
  Recipe 4, 87-88
  Recipe 5, 88
  Recipe 6, 89

S
Sherry, making, basic
method, 25
  flor, 24-25
  gypsum, role in making, 24
  recipes
    oloroso sherry 1, 28
    oloroso sherry 2, sweet, 29
    oloroso sherry 3, 29
    oloroso sherry 4, 30
    oloroso sherry 5,
     full-bodied, 31
    original dry fino sherry
     1, 25-26
    dry fino sherry 2, 26
    dry fino sherry 3, 26-27
    dry fino sherry 4, 27
    dry fino sherry 5, 27-28
Silberwasser
  Recipe, 117
Sloe Gin, 123
Strega, 123
Sulfur dioxide, role in
winemaking, 19-20

T
Troubleshooting, 20-21

V
Vermouth, 123-124

W
White wine
  Basic method, 60-61
  Types
    Bordeaux Blanc, recipe, 67
    Burgundy, white
      Recipe 1, 61

      Recipe 2, 62
      Recipe 3, 62
    Chablis, 58-59
      Recipe, 61
    Graves, 59
      Recipe 1, 64
      Recipe 2, 64-65
      Recipe 3, 65
      Recipe 4, 65
      Recipe 5, 66
    Montrachet, 57-58
    Pouilly-Fuissé, 58
    Sauternes, 58-59
      Recipe 1, 63
      Recipe 2, 63
      Recipe 3, 64
Wines
  alcohol table, 105
  ease in making, 100-101
  preparing, 105
  taste testing, 106

More Great Books from Fox Chapel Publishing

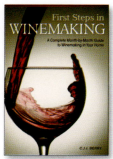

First Steps in Winemaking
A Complete Month-by-Month Guide to Winemaking in Your Home
By C. J. J. Berry

Delve into the world of at-home winemaking with methods and techniques that will turn your kitchen into a vineyard.

ISBN: 978-1-56523-602-8
$14.95 • 240 Pages

130 New Winemaking Recipes
Make Delicious Wine at Home Using Fruits, Grains, and Herbs
By C. J. J. Berry

Follow these 130 classic recipes for making wine in your own kitchen using traditional country ingredients.

ISBN: 978-1-56523-600-4
$12.95 • 136 Pages

Winemaking with Concentrates
How to Make Delicious Wines at Home with Easy-to-Use Fruit Concentrates
By Peter Duncan

This book is for the winemaker who likes the ease and convenience of making wine from concentrates, or for those who enjoy wine but lack the facilities to make it from grapes and other fruits.

ISBN: 978-1-56523-676-9
$12.95 • 96 Pages

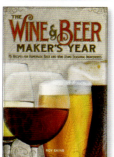

The Wine and Beer Maker's Year
75 Recipes for Homemade Beer and Wine Using Seasonal Ingredients
By Roy Elkins

A round-the-year guide to wine and beer making, covering dry and sweet wines, beers, lagers, liqueurs, and fortified wines.

ISBN: 978-1-56523-675-2
$12.95 • 160 Pages

Look for These Books at Your Local Retailer

To order direct, call **800-457-9112** or visit *www.FoxChapelPublishing.com*
By mail, please send check or money order + S&H to:
Fox Chapel Publishing, 1970 Broad Street, East Petersburg, PA 17520

# Item	Shipping Rate	
1 Item	$3.99 US	$8.98 CAI
Each Additional	.99 US	$3.99 CAI

International Orders - please email info@foxchapelpublishing.com or visit our website for actual shipping costs.